Dating for Engineers

Denis O'Sullivan
Daniel T. Chen

Brussels - Dublin - Saint Paul - Düsseldorf

ISBN 978-0-6152-2283-7

To Purchase more copies of this Book:

This book is available for purchase online at www.lulu.com, we think the ID is 865592 but we're not sure. If that doesn't work, search by booktitle or author.

At the time of going to press (roughly 3.15 pm), there are still many otherwise fine bookstores who do not plan to stock it ..

This photo shows an engineer talking to some women. For obvious reasons this had to be faked, as no women were willing to be photographed near an engineer. You'd expect that being engineers, we'd have found a really clever way to fake this using Photoshop or CAD – but in fact it was achieved by a combination of simple trigonometry, alcohol and the choice of the right people, and we think the technique might be instructive for those whose credibilty might be improved by being seen (in photos only) in the company of real women.

In the photo you appear to see a reasonably tall engineer talking to two average height ladies. In reality the engineer is 4'3" (1m28) tall, while the two women are each well over 6' (1.83m) tall, and that's without the heels they're both wearing. He did actually try to talk to them, but within 24 hours they had obtained a restraining order, forcing him to remain at least 50m (165 feet) away from them.

However, by placing the camera just 2'(0.61m) off the ground (and obviously hiding it from the women), and by providing them with enough cuba libre to make them smile ceaselessly, we were able to take this photograph by having our engineer standing 50m away, on the straight line between the camera and the women who, for legal reason as mentioned above, were a further 50m away.

By wearing a black t-shirt, it was easy to superimpose the women's arms on his chest to make it appear that they were equidistant from the camera and actually embracing him. Then it was just a case of superimposing an interior location on the background and numerically reworking the photograph with Photoshop (OK, so we did have to use it in the end ...). The only thing ruining the effect is the engineer's inability to remove the beer from his hand for even the duration of a photo.

So, if when you finish this book you feel that you've been cheated in some way, it's worth remembering that it's extremely unlikely that any royalties the authors might receive for this book will even come close to covering their legal costs if these two women ever see the book and sue them.

Preface by Pope Innocent X

Not many people know this, but before being pope, I was an engineer. In those days it was a tough training, not like nowadays when computers do all the work. And this brief experience had a lasting impact on my life, and makes me particularly qualified to endorse this fine volume.

Indeed, while there were obviously some spiritual motivations for my becoming a man of the cloth, I would be lying if I denied that my total inability to attract women as an engineer made the vow of chastity a lot less of an issue than it might otherwise have been.

And now, being Pope, and therefore almost by definition a Roman Catholic, I obviously spend a lot of time thinking about sex. And in this context I find this book to be a particularly valuable contribution not only to the clarification of the Vatican's position on sexual intercourse, but also to its implementation. The authors have clearly found a new and original way to address a subject which has for many years troubled those of us who desire to limit sexual intercourse to the use intended by God, namely for reproduction inside a marriage blessed by the Holy Roman Catholic Church, in order to produce the next generation of Catholics.

The originality of their approach lies not in forbidding intercourse, or even in forbidding contraception, as successive generations of Catholic leaders have done and will no doubt do in future, but rather by encouraging those seeking to engage in extramarital sex to pursue a strategy which is from the outset doomed to failure, but whose inevitable futility is camouflaged through the use of relatively incomprehensible mathematical analysis, much of which hasn't even been invented at the time I'm writing this.

It is therefore with great pleasure that I give this book my wholehearted approval as yet another weapon which, along with the Spanish Inquisition, the Crusades and so forth, some of which may have happened after my death, depending on when I actually lived, will keep the people of the planet on course for salvation.

Yours Faithfully

Pope Innocent X

PS before you discount my opinion, look at the huge statue of me in the Vatican. When I see your statue in the Vatican, then I might listen to what you say.

Authors' Preface

There are those who dedicate their lives to making the world a better place. Then there are those who recognize that a life of gluttony and sloth is a more realistic personal objective.

Analogously, there are books which aim to change the course of history through their penetrating insights, peerless analysis and compelling conclusions. And there are books like this one.

As an Engineering undergraduate textbook, this material is most appropriately covered as a two-semester course, ideally split between sophomore and senior year. The core of the material in chapters 0-12 should be covered in the sophomore year, with the more mathematical and technical discussions in chapters 13-17 being saved for the senior year. This division is rendered practical by the fact that the material in chapter 13 and beyond is targeted primarily at engineers who have, at some point in the past, had some experience of dating.

Some reviewers have suggested that the material may also be appropriate, perhaps in a more simplified form, for students of the physical and biological sciences, mathematics, logic and French. We leave it decision at the discretion of each course-designer to ascertain whether the students will have the appropriate combination of mathematical sophistication and social ineptitude which make the text so valuable for engineers.

As a graduate-level textbook, we believe it should be possible to cover all the material in one semester, and in this case there is little doubt that much of the material will be both relevant and helpful to gradual students in many other scientific and non-scientific disciplines.

One vexing question which dogged previous editions of this text has been the appropriateness of the course for female students. In Japan, this text is published with "Not for sale to Women!" in large red letters on the cover – or more precisely in large red Kanji. In Wales, we were only allowed to sell the text if 10% of the profits were donated to the Society for the Care and Welfare of Psychologically Damaged Sheep. On the other hand, in Sweden the text had to be translated in a completely gender neutral manner. Since in many cases this was effectively logically impossible, we rejected all responsibility for this and had the translation done by computer, and the book now sells primarily as an auto-repair manual for owners of unhappy Volvo's.

In the text, we have frequently, and sometimes necessarily, focused on the somewhat stereotypical male engineer. While this may be considered a limitation, in a sense this is justified by the fact that it is ~~we~~ they who typically have the most difficulty interacting with normal people, and especially with women. Female engineers at least get to live in a predominantly male environment, and while they are undoubtedly far from socially adapted, in our experience they do not usually display the full range of social inadequacy which one observes in the male engineer. So it could be argued that they have less need of this material. That said, the vast majority of the material can readily be read, understood and applied by any student regardless both of his/her gender and of the gender of his/her desired partner.

The authors are immensely indebted to a lot of people for making this work possible. Actually, come to think of it, nobody has helped us at all. So forget that. We would, though, like to extend a profound appreciation to Dr. Tim Laska, who has so kindly volunteered to appear, often anonymously, in so many of the examples.

If there is one element of irony in the whole project, it is in the fact that, having set out to write a book that would be both largely inaccessible and highly impractical – and obviously, totally useless – we have discovered (seriously) that this wasn't actually possible. In those chapters in which rigorous mathematical analysis has been applied to problems normally considered the domain of philosophy, psychology or social science, we were surprised to find that the results were genuinely interesting. Even in cases where the mathematical result was somewhat cumbersome, the underlying principles offered clear and sometimes unexpected insights.

Or maybe we just made that bit up. You'll have to decide for yourself.

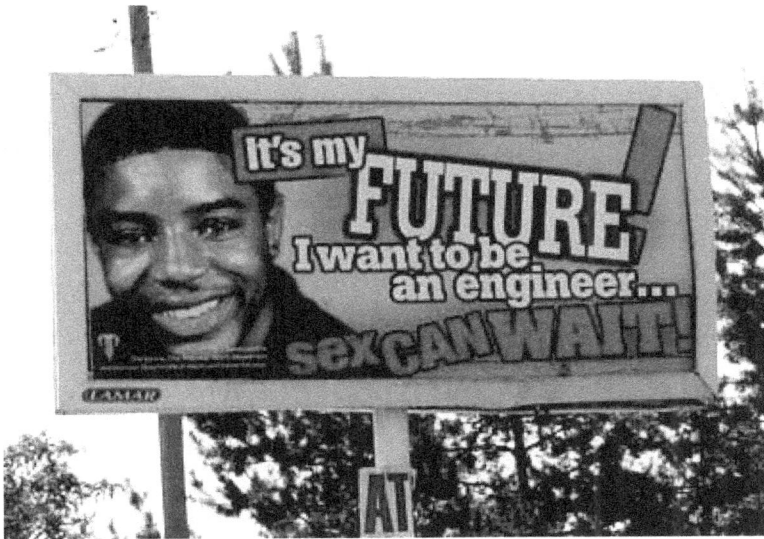

This billboard sums up the problem faced by engineers. Notice that it doesn't specify exactly how long sex will have to wait. And unfortunately, for many of those who choose engineering, that can be a long long time ... (sorry we can't find out who took this photo to give credit)

Dating for Engineers – Contents

Introduction: Why You Need this Book

This is not a book to help engineers (or scientists) find life-partners, although that may be a side-effect (*caveat emptor* – we accept no legal responsibility if this should happen). This book has the much more challenging goal of helping engineers to be cool in the eyes of female[1] colleagues and friends, so that they become the one the cutest colleagues want to sleep with, so that they become the guy who meets the coolest women in bars and clubs – in other words, so that they achieve the sex-life they've always wanted.

We realise that this sounds like a tall order, but it's not just an idle boast – the text includes full, valid, mathematical proofs of why the techniques we present will work. If you find a flaw in the proofs of any of the theorems presented, we will be happy to publish your correction in the next edition.

Historically engineers, and to a lesser extent, scientists, have rarely been associated freely in the female mind with sex[2], except perhaps in the context of being suitable providers with whom to raise a family after the wild sexual appetite has been satisfied. There are many reasons for this, but perhaps principal among them is that the typical engineer has the social interactions skills of a dung beetle at a hypochondriacs conference.[3]

---

[1] Already in the first paragraph it's been pointed out by one of the foolish volunteers who read through this that we've sometimes assumed that all engineers are male, and at other times made inadequate, politically-correct attempts to appear to write in a non-gender-specific way and provide useful advice and analysis for both men and women engineers. After careful consideration, we the authors have decided that this apparently inadvertent inconsistency is actually a complex and insightful metaphor for the inconsistency with which all male engineers consider the needs of women, which is one of the central messages of this text. Anyhow, we think that women engineers who are wise enough to purchase this book will easily be able to adapt the lessons to their own needs, as indeed should gays, lesbians and hermaphrodites.

[2] Dunphy, Jones, Smith, "Physiological and psychological consequences of social incompetence among engineers", *J. Ch. E. S.,* 1968

[3] Although it has also been argued that dress- and fashion-sense play a role, by Wilson in his famous 1981 article "Emasculation through pocket-protectors"

Now, at least some engineers are somewhat aware of their deficiencies in this area, in the sense that they sometimes hear non-engineers speaking about something called sex, and seeming rather excited about it, but find themselves callously rebuffed when they ask some female to participate in a fact-finding experiment with them.

And, given that most engineers have a lot of disposable income, many books have been written with the intention of capturing some of that disposable income in return for a vague promise that following the book's recipe will result in an ability to potentially function semi-normally in social situations, and perhaps eventually even to have a relationship with a (very patient and not very demanding) female.

This book is no different in its goal of capturing some of the engineers' disposable income for its very deserving authors, but differs in important ways. Previous books have focused on trying to help the engineer achieve basic competence in areas such as conversation, wearing the correct number of shoes, matching said shoes and, for more advanced engineers, matching said shoes with trousers and socks of not totally incompatible colours (the well known "don't mix blue, brown and orange" rule comes from a 1973 Danish text-book for engineers by Hansen and Hansen).

We believe that there are two fundamental problems with the above approach. First, there is extremely strong evidence (e.g. you bought this book) that it doesn't work. But second, it neglects the most basic difference between engineers and non-engineers – a difference so important that we shall name it:

The fundamental Axiom of Engineers

Engineers are much smarter that non-engineers.   *Ax   0.1*

The proof of this is left as an exercise for the reader.

We've called it an axiom not only because we hold it to be self-evident, but also because it leaves the field open for our sequel, "non-Euclidean Dating for Engineers", which will follow from allowing for cases where this axiom does not hold, including the effects of dating in a space-time continuum where the intelligence of Business majors is non-negligible[4] - a

---

[4] Important to note here that the intelligence referred to is that of others competing for the same scarce resource (heterosexual women), which will be primarily other males. It is always best policy to regard any women as being smarter than both engineers and male

concept that is hard to imagine for anyone who's ever worked with Marketers or Management Consultants. The practical consequences of this are sufficiently remote for us to ignore it at this stage.[5]

Corollaries of the fundamental axiom of Engineers are many, and will recur throughout the text, but in this introduction we will focus on one. To illustrate, consider the example of a 7', 340 lb engineer who dreams of becoming a jockey and winning the Kentucky Derby. The traditional engineer-help books have adopted an approach analogous to putting him on a diet, so that after a couple of years he's a demoralised 7', 240 lb failed jockey. This book proposes focusing on the engineers' advantages rather than trying to fix the problems. In the case of the 7' engineer, we would propose to him to join the NBA, use his height to become a star and earn hundreds of millions of dollars, until eventually he'd be able to afford a very strong horse and have enough left over to pay off all the other jockeys in the Derby.

It should probably be pointed out at this stage that we do not see it as our role to provide moral guidance. However one can easily sketch a proof justifying almost any act of treachery if the net result is to pass on more engineer-genes and fewer genes belonging to Marketers or Lawyers. This again is left as an exercise for the overly-conscientious reader.

Perhaps that illustration served more to confuse than clarify. So let's just state the corollary:

Corollary 1

Engineers' best chance of success is to use their intelligence,   *C 0.1*
rather than trying vainly to match non-engineers in areas in
which they are simply not competent to do so.

This book demonstrates the methods by which this can be achieved. While the tone is not always reverent, and occasional references are

---

non-engineers. Hartford (*J. Ch. E. S.* 1994) has investigated the paradoxical case of female engineers, and has shown conclusively that female engineers, *quà* females, are smarter than female engineers, *quà* engineers, therby validating our hypothesis. Hartford himself, in a footnote to his famous article, indicated that while his proof was convincing, he had absolutely no idea what the conclusion meant, but in the tradition of engineering literature, that was no reason not to publish it.

[5] It has been postulated that at times less than 10^{-43}s after the big bang, some Business majors were actually quite smart, but since at that time it was far too hot for sex, we will not worry about it.

apocryphal, the objective is deadly serious, in the broadest sense of the term, sort of, and after reading the book, you (if you're smart enough to understand it) will believe this too.

In terms of reading, the chapters are in a somewhat logical order, but with few exceptions, it is possible to read chapters independently. For example, Chapter 16 deals with the solution to question of how to recognize when you've maxed out (you're not going to find a better woman and so it'd be smart to settle down if she's willing) – if there are engineers who already find themselves in this situation, they may skip directly to this chapter, with only some optional brief pre-reading of the n-dimensional vector field approach to partner evaluation in Chapter 11 needed to gain a full understanding of the material in Chapter 16.

Since the first of the Natural Numbers is 0 and not 1, obviously we start with Chapter 0, which is intended as a slight morale boost which will probably be needed to deal with some of the material which follows.

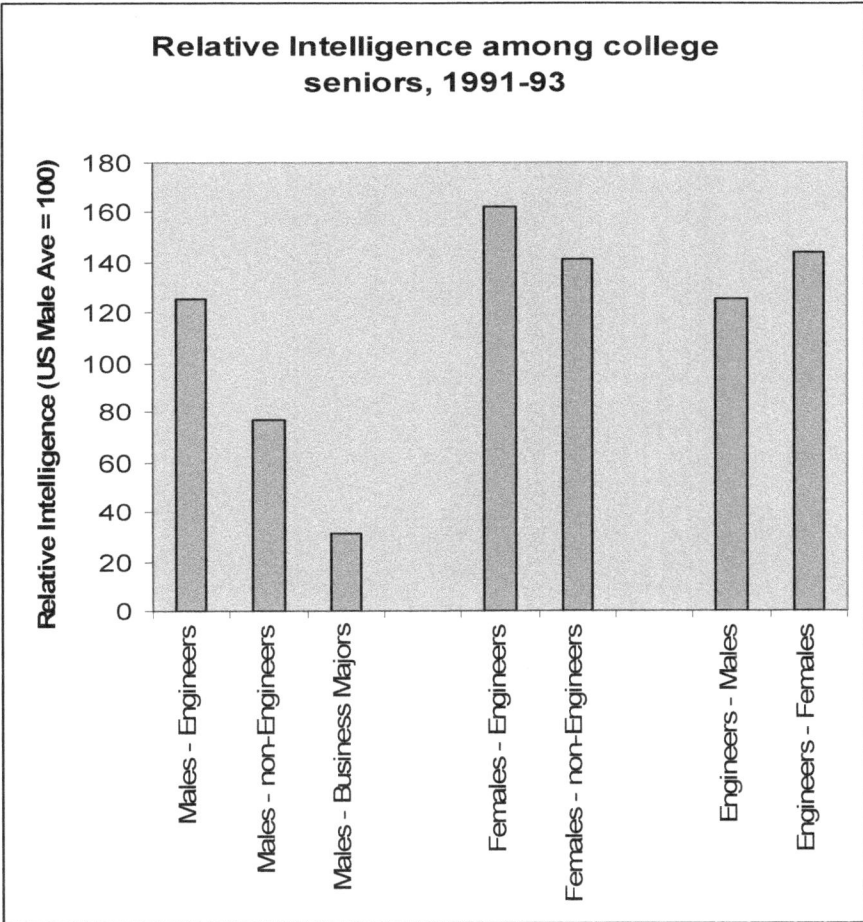

Figure 0.1 The topline results from Hartford's breakthrough results from a study of over 30,000 seniors at US universities in the years 1991-93 (see Footnote previous page). Like many famous results of quantum theory, his findings have been confirmed by subsequent studies, but nobody has yet understood how exactly the same test-data for women Engineers give different averages depending on whether the women are primarily categorized as "women" or as "engineers".

Section A: Preliminaries

On Why You Deserve More than You're Getting

Chapter 0   A Real-life Example – Bob and Marsha

This chapter has been included at the insistence of our publisher, who questions the gullibility of our target audience, and suggests they will need some evidence early on that there is something in this book for them. So, without conceding ground on the question of gullibility – remember cold-fusion, the England football team, . . . – we did accept the potential desirability of demonstrating upfront how the techniques we're going to discuss can work in real life.

Consider the following situation:

ACME Inc. hires the beautiful and single architect, Marsha, to its head-office, immediately creating a race among all the single (and some not-so-single) men in the company. Among these are the usual mix of well-dressed marketers with cool cars, rich accountants in 3-piece suits, "creatively-dressed" advertising developers who smoke pot at work, jocks with great hair racing up the management ladder and so on. And there's also Bob the engineer, with a rusty 1987 Ford Fiesta (it still gets great mileage), a beer-belly and more hairs on his back than on his head – which are clearly visible through is collection of vintage 1984 shirts with huge yellow marks under the arms.

At first sight, the uninformed observer might be tempted to say that Bob isn't in with a chance of winning the fair Marsha's heart – or at least of sleeping with her a few times. But if Bob has read this book and taken its key lessons to heart, all is not lost. Now, we're not saying that he's guaranteed to win her every time – just that there are steps he can take to turn himself into a front-runner – at which point he may need to re-read our chapter about making some minimal effort on personal appearance if he wants to complete the conquest.

How is Bob to achieve this? The key is very simple. He must stop thinking of interaction with Marsha as social (and therefore, awkward, unpleasant, nerve-inducing and to be avoided), and must instead focus on the situation as he would on any other difficult/ impossible engineering problem. This is again so fundamental that we call it

---

The First Theorem of Engineers and Sex

The problem of (not) getting laid can be addressed in a similar manner to that which works in the case of a car that   *Th 0.1* won't start or of a distillation column that's only achieving 56% plate efficiency when it's designed to achieve 65%. (However, the specific calculations required may differ.)

Proof

We show that each problem can be stated in the same general form and that the solution of each can follow a similar path. It is for the solver to find the actual solution in each case – and the more difficult the challenge, the more advantageous becomes the engineer's superior problem-solving ability:

Existing situation = State A (given)

Desired situation = State B (given)

Objective: define and follow strategy to reach State B from State A.

Additional Constraints may or may not be present (e.g. limited expenditure).

The problem may also be stated in the form of optimisation (e.g. as fast as possible, as cheaply as possible, ….)

Strategies consist of functions which may be applied to elements of State A or of intermediate states which lead to reaching State B. (e.g. remove sludge from the distillation column, buy flowers)

To consider the specific problem of Bob, we have (reducing the number of variables for clarity, with no loss of generality):

State A (initial conditions):
- Marsha joins company on May 1st, 2006
- Interested parties are:
  - Bob,
  - Henry the rich Accountant,
  - Joe the high-flying manager with great hair,
  - Fran the Marketer with a cool car and nice clothes,
  - Olivier the French Advertising Developer.
- For simplicity, we assume that Marsha is new in town, and that for 3 months she will not meet anyone interesting outside work. (poor woman). So time-limit is July 31st 2006.

State B (desired outcome – boundary condition at $t = 3$ *months*)
Bob and Marsha are sleeping together regularly (without any direct cash payment involved).

Once he views the situation in this format, Bob is immediately more at ease. Following some of the techniques outlined later in this book, he will first re-state his objective in terms of individually achievable goals, which, combined, will lead to the desired situation. For example, these goals might be:

- Marsha must be convinced that sleeping with someone at work is a good idea, despite all evidence to the contrary. Once that's achieved, the next goal is easily stated:
- She must prefer to sleep with Bob than with Olivier, Fran, Joe or Henry and/or they must decide they no longer want to sleep with her. (four separate goals).

Once she's convinced, Bob must not screw up actually asking her out.

Already, each of these goals begins to seem much less impossible than the original challenge.

And interestingly, each of the other four candidates will be facing exactly the same challenge, more or less.

The situation is shown diagramatically on the next page:

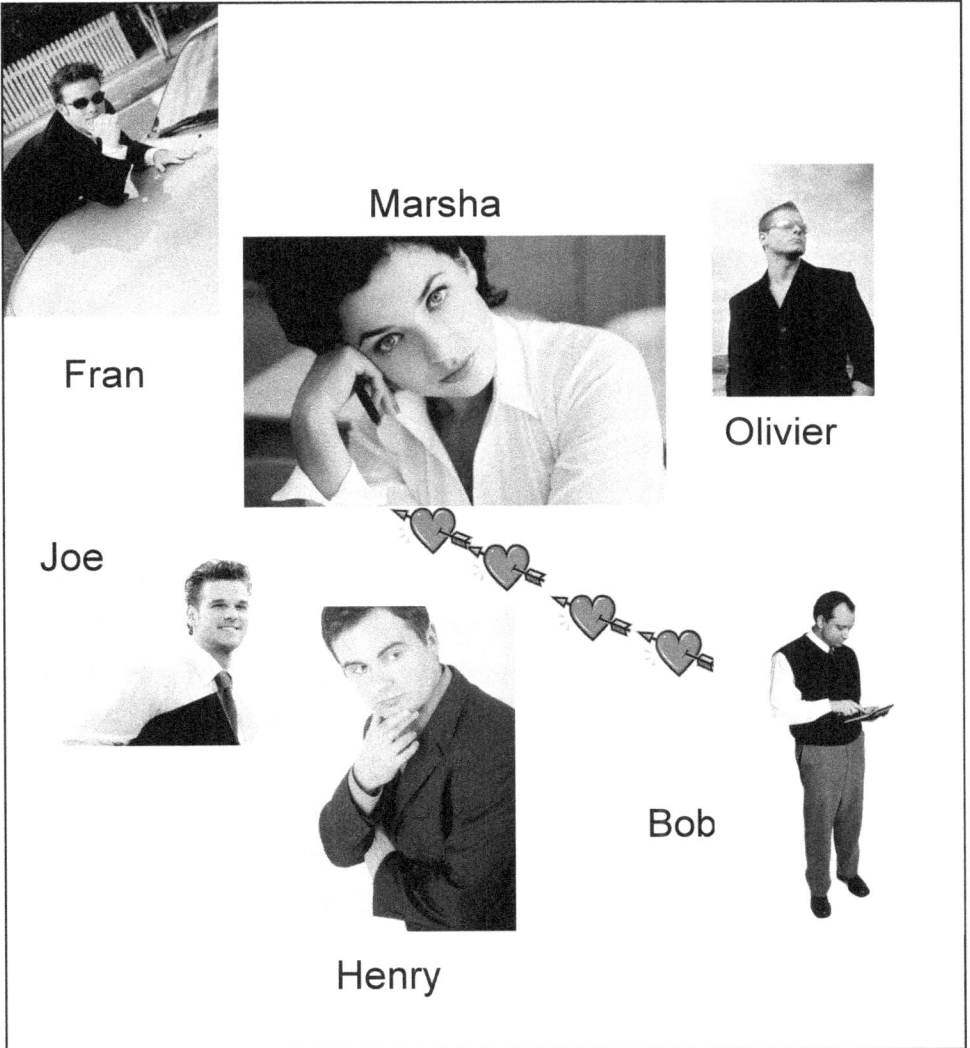

Figure 0.1 The Marsha Problem

It is at this point that Bob must apply his one advantage over the others – his superior intelligence and problem-solving ability. Because, being an engineer, he's actually smarter than they are. Or, to quote the theorem as it is stated in Perry's *Handbook of Chemical Engineering*:

The Theorem of Engineers and non-Engineers

Most non-engineers are not very bright.[6]   *Th 0.2*

By the time he's read this book, Bob will be able to put this kind of important new knowledge, and a host of winning strategies, to use in order to get laid more often by women like Marsha. And ultimately, Marsha too will be a winner (in the broader sense of the term ....). In fact, we treat a very similar example to this in the chapter on Competitive Dating Situations.

And now, without further ado, let's begin with the first real chapter, which logically deals with statistics.

[With no disrespect to the authors, though, I should point out that the chapter on statistics is an exceptionally dull chapter, even by the standards of this book, so you may in fact be better advised to skip to the following chapter. – Editor's Note]

[Actually, it was so dull that in this revised addition, we've moved it to the appendix, so unless you're hopelessly inept with stats (e.g. did you major in Business Studies?), you probably don't need to read it before continuing to Chapter 1 – Editor's Second Note].

---

[6] Perry's goes on to say: "You probably think you know some pretty dim engineers. But if you venture out into the world of non-engineers, you will be amazed. You will think these people are being ironic, using a code you don't understand, working in base-12 or whatever. But sooner or later, if you want to learn to deal with Marketers, Accountants, Lawyers, etc., you have to face facts. These people are dim. Until you accept this conjecture as the only possible explanation for their behaviour, you will have difficulties dealing with them."

Chapter 1   Statistical Proof That You Ought to be Having More Sex (n ≥ 110)

If you've bought this book, or received it as a gift, that may indicate that your success in the dating world has to date been somewhat limited. In future chapters we will discuss the key mathematical techniques you will need to use in order to improve your success rate. However, to begin, we present a brief statistical analysis of your current situation, and demonstrate the extraordinarily high probability that your situation has the potential to improve. Reassuringly, both deductive and inductive analyses lead to the same conclusion, and experiment seems to confirm its validity. Once you're fully convinced of the immensely improbable nature of your current predicament, for such it is, it will be trivial[7] to quantum-tunnel your way back into the more probable state of normal existence and regular sex to which you'd like to become accustomed.

An introduction for those who have forgotten absolutely everything they ever knew about statistics (a prerequisite for entering corporate management), appears as an appendix. For the following discussion, it is assumed that the reader has a working understanding of the Null Hypothesis and basic statistics.

Exciting, isn't it? Well, anyway, let's get to the analysis.

---

[7] As in standard engineering textbooks, the word trivial is occasionally used to indicate "almost impossible" as in the phrase "the proof of this conjecture is trivial and is left as an exercise for the student".

Analysis of your current situation: 1 - Inductive Approach

The full inductive proof is beyond the scope of this book, delving as it does into complex areas of cellular biochemistry and evolutionary biology. However, a somewhat less rigorous inductive argument is still extremely convincing.

(for non-engineering readers, induction is a process used to derive conclusions based on what went before, while deduction is used to derive conclusions based on axioms agreed to be true. A full inductive proof that the sun will rise tomorrow would have two parts:

  1. The sun rose today
  2. If the sun rises on day n, then it will also rise on day $n+1$.

Now, without getting into very complex astrophysics, and probably not even then, you can't actually prove the second part of this – in fact, we know that one day the sun will explode and become a red giant and it will not "rise" because it will have engulfed the earth. But still, based on a very long historical number of occasions on which the sun has risen, we can state with a very high degree of probability that the sun will indeed rise tomorrow, without necessarily understanding the astrophysics at all. The proof offered below is of a similar nature, not rigorous, but nonetheless very convincing).

There are two alternative theories of how we all come to be here at all. One theory holds that we've evolved over millions of years. The other holds that we are descended from Adam and Eve, who were created some 6000 years ago. In the sequel to this book, we can discuss the merits of these two theories, but for the moment (and this is already somewhat improbable), we're going to prove that, independently of which of these theories is true, it is likely that you should be having "biblical relations" with the opposite sex more often than you are.

Because, whichever theory you choose, you need to add a hypothesis as to how the billions of people who are alive today descended from a very small number many years ago. And both biblical scholars and Darwinians concur that the central aspect of this hypothesis will almost certainly involve a lot of people, throughout history, having sexual intercourse with each other. With the exception of one disputed case in Israel some 2000 years ago, in fact, these scholars agree that nobody has lived who was not the result of some form of sexual act. So, this means:

Theorem of Other People and Sex

Lots and lots of people are having lots and lots of sex, or else   *Th 1.1*
there wouldn't be all these people around.

But studies have shown that it goes further than that. Because, as the saying goes, virginity is hereditary, and therefore

---

Theorem of your Ancestors and Sex

You come from a line of people, going back at least 6011   *Th 1.2*
years, who had sexual intercourse at least once.

Let's look at the more difficult case, namely the literal Biblical interpretation, in which you are descended from Adam and Eve, who lived about 6000 years ago. Even with the very conservative estimate that each of your ancestors was born when their parents were about 30, that still means that there have been 200 generations between you and Adam and Eve. And in each of those generations, all of your (biological) ancestors performed at least one successful act of sexual intercourse. Yes, your 2 parents, your 4 grandparents, your 8 great-grandparents, and so on!! All of them !! Every one.[8]

So, logically, if I were to propose the "null hypothesis" that your family history suggests that you mightn't be very successful at sex, you could point to this very impressive statistic to put me in my place. How many people exactly is that. Well, if we assume that you are not in some sense in-bred, that would be quite a large number – at the time of Adam and Eve, we'd be talking about 2 to the power of 200, which would be about 10 to the power of 60. So, I think we'll all have to accept that there was some in-breeding in our history, which also goes quite a way towards explaining some of the people who get elected to Congress.

Rather than play around with assumptions which might be questionable, let's assume the absolutely most conservative case, namely that in each

---

[8] Unless of course Dan Brown is right *and* you happen to be descended from the Virgin Mary, in which case, this assumption isn't strictly exact, but still accurate to well below 1%.

generation of your family, the parents were siblings. Outside some of the southern US, this is probably somewhat unrealistic, but that just makes the numbers below even stronger.

So 200 generations of 2 siblings each copulating with each other, that's 400 ancestors altogether, and each one of them had sex at least once.

But of course that's only scratching the surface. Because we're talking about successful cases. We must ask ourselves, how much sex they must have had to *ensure* one successful outcome. Again, taking the church as our reference, in this case the tried and trusted method of natural contraception, we can conclude that over a typical month, most acts of intercourse are unlikely to result in conception. So, even assuming (against the evidence) that everything went well every time, we still would have only about a 1 in 5 chance of it being the right time of the month. And with pestilence and plagues and cannibalism and all the other things that your ancestors went through, the chances of a fertilised egg growing into a 30-year old adult were certainly no better than 25% (you can dispute this, it only changes the numbers slightly, so I went for a simple round number). So combining these two, your ancestors had at most a 1 in 20 chance of conceiving someone who would grow up to be 30 years old and ready to further the chain.

Does this mean that they had sexual intercourse at least 20 times? Well, if you weren't an engineer, you might think that, but the reality is much more interesting:

Let's say we want to create a situation in which you personally have a 50% chance of existing, which was surely what Adam and Eve were thinking about all those years ago. Considering that as a reasonable starting axiom, a little anthropocentric perhaps, this means that the total probability of conception for all of 200 consecutive generations must be at least 50%. Let's assume that the probability is about the same for each generation (this is intended as a simple book), and that the probability of conception is p. Then, this reduces to:

$$p^{200} > 0.5$$

or

$$p = 0.99654$$

Now, if every time you have sex, you have (at most!!) only a 5% probability of producing a surviving, reproducing offspring, how often do you need to have sex to be 99.654% sure of conceiving at least once? Again, a trivial matter for the statistician:

Let n be the number of times. The easiest way to answer the question is to think of the contrary situation: Every time they had sex, there was a 95% chance that they would *not* conceive and produce a child who would go on to reach 30. So, even if they had sex 20 times, the chances that they would not have conceived would be

$$prob \ = \ 0.95^{20} \ = \ 0.36$$

Yes, even having sex 20 times, there's a 1 in 3 chance that they would not have produced any surviving children. But we need the chance of failure to conceive to be much lower, namely $1 - 0.99654$, or 0.346 %. So we'd have:

$$0.00346 \ = \ 0.95^{n}$$

Working this out, $n = 110$.

In other words, you are descended from a line of 400 people, each of whom most likely had sex[9] at least 100 times during their fertile years (yes, 100 isn't exactly a spectacular number, but it's probably better than you're doing at the moment). This despite the fact that they didn't have cars or James Taylor CD's or toothpaste or deodorant.

So logically, the statistical likelihood that you don't have the genetic capacity to do at least that well is very low[10].

Analysis of your current situation: 2 - Deductive Approach

A deductive approach would be to calculate from first principles how regularly you should be getting laid. This is much easier than the previous derivation.

First we need some key axioms. History has shown that Euclid's axiom about parallel lines prevented him from discovering non-Euclidean geometry, but Euclid himself would doubtless say that had he not had this axiom, there would be no need for the terms Euclidean and non-Euclidean, and so nobody would ever have heard of him. [Newton himself had a similar observation about his assumption of the linear stress-strain relationship in fluids, especially after foolishly choosing to have an SI

---

[9] with somebody else

[10] there is one minor flaw in this inductive proof, as you've surely spotted. If not, maybe this isn't the book for you. The flaw is in the somewhat immodest assumption that 200 generations have lived with the sole objective of producing exactly you, even though they couldn't possibly have known what you'd be like; if they had, surely at least one generation would have made the sacrifice of celibacy. But the gist of the conclusion, that all your ancestors had sex regularly, is probably close to the truth.

unit[11] which almost nobody uses named after him, when there were so many options still open to him].

These axioms however do not admit any doubt:

Fundamental Axioms of Sex

There are lots of people out there who are not having sex right now.   *Ax 1.1*

Many of them would rather be having sex right now than what they're doing.   *Ax 1.2*

The second one, in particular, comes as a major surprise to many male engineers. So it's worth repeating specifically for them, in a slightly simpler format. Even women like sex. (If they didn't, it's hard to imagine which of the other aspects of childbearing would have convinced them to procreate over the aeons). It is difficult to comprehend for the typical male mind, and doubly so for the male engineer. How is he supposed to struggle and strategize and compete for something when the "opponent" is more than willing to accede to his desires? And why, if women are so desirous of sex, do they so effectively hide this when approached by engineers?

Now, it would be trivializing the situation to say that you just have to go up to the next woman you see who isn't having sex and ask her to sleep with you. Because there is a problem. You have to ask *nicely*. And in our sequel we're going to define nicely. For the moment, we're just going to make the simple deduction from the two axioms above that there is an enormous opportunity for you to get more sex than you've ever imagined, and all you need to do is work out how.

Logically, this is a problem, and you're an engineer, so you should be better at this than (fill in the name of some dimwit friend who gets laid more often than you). This pretty much proves that the situation you're currently in is a highly improbable one, certainly it's thermodynamically unstable – if you can work out how to break the symmetry, you could be enjoying regular sex[12] for years to come.

But this whole statistics bit is getting rather tedious[13], let's move onto something more interesting.

---

[11] the Newton – again, we apologize to non Business majors for this patronizing footnote.
[12] with somebody else
[13] incidentally, our experience is that many women find the whole area of statistics tedious, and that as dinner conversatoin on a date, it ranks only above Quality Assurance and your personal physiological problems.

Section B: Reality

On Why You Are Where You Are

Chapter 2   You, the Engineer. Take a Look at Yourself

Before you can even start thinking about how to convince somebody to sleep with you, it's important that you fully understand yourself, take a long hard look at yourself, your mind, your body, your qualities, your defects, the attributes you possess which might make you appealing to members of the opposite sex.

On second thoughts maybe that's not such a good idea.

Chapter 3   You, the Engineer – Really, Take a Long Hard Look at Yourself

No, unfortunately this self-analysis bit is necessary, however painful it may be.

To help you out, we've provided some typical characteristics of engineers. Not all engineers possess all these characteristics, or at least many successfully delude themselves for years that they don't.

The authors would like to thank Dr. Tim Laska for agreeing to appear in the examples described below.

Section 1 – Physical Pulchritude among Engineers

This is not our forte. And this is unfortunate, because physical attractiveness is one of the few characteristics which really helps a person get laid.

A simplistic view might lead us to conclude that statistically engineers should be more or less as attractive as everyone else. But there are several fairly straightforward, mathematically valid reasons why this is not the case:

1. While some people might study engineering out of pure desire or nerdiness, choosing to work twice as hard as students in any other faculty to end up in low-paying jobs with long hours just for the pure intellectual satisfaction of it, for most of us this was not the case. Consider a simple equation in which our average day (or week, or month) during college is divided by the time spent pursuing different activities:

$$t_{study} + t_{sleep} + t_{sports} + t_{socialising} + \ldots = t_{total} \quad \text{(e.g. 24 hours)}$$

First, look at the pre-decision phase. The student knows that engineering involves more work than other faculties. Students with active sport or social lives therefore shy away from engineering, while those without social lives, without sporting interests, tend towards it. The relative value of the additional time to be spent studying is much less relevant to the latter group, so while it won't be true in every case, on average those who choose engineering will be those who have less active social-lives and are less involved in sporting activity.

Let's look at what this means. Attractive people almost invariably have full social lives, due to the social desirability of beauty and other people's desire to associate with them. Very unattractive people frequently do not have very active social lives, for the same reason. [It is a tragedy of modern society that the level of discrimination against unattractive people is so high, and yet fully condoned, but as stated previously we're not here to moralise.] Therefore, in general, people with less active social-lives will be less attractive than average.

Now consider sports. Sports are one of the few ways to improve physical attractiveness, by at least improving the physical attractiveness of the physique. Again on average, those who do sports will tend to be fitter, leaner, closer to the ideal body shape (for men or women) and therefore more attractive.

So, by attracting students with less active social lives and who are less active in sports, engineering is attracting a group of people who are *already significantly less attractive than the average, even before they start to study engineering*. And this conclusion is not based on any stereotypes about nerds with pocket protectors.

Now, let's consider the 4 years of college. While the other students continue their sports, so getting fitter and stronger, while the other students continue their social lives, while the other students get their "beauty sleep", the engineer is quite likely to be working on his process thermodynamics or finishing his lab report. All of which serves only to increase the pulchritude gap between engineers and normal students.

But even this isn't everything. Because there is one aspect of social life at which engineers (in their own eyes) excel, and that is the art of drinking lots and lots of beer. The effects of beer on male beauty are well known and need not be discussed here – this is just one more factor in the sad decline in physical attractiveness that besets the engineer during his college years.

2. So it is certainly true that by the time of graduation, the base material with which the engineer has to work (i.e. his body) is well below average. But that's still only part of the problem. Because during the years of college, the engineer has also fallen behind the rest of the world in terms of other aspects of physical appearance, such as personal hygiene, dress sense and personal grooming. When you see someone wearing brown sandals with knee-length black socks and red shorts strolling across campus, you know it's an engineer.

In our effort to be rigid in our derivations in this book, we have to be honest and admit that the scientific explanation of this phenomenon is far from conclusive. It would again be easy to fall into easy stereotypes – *à la* the scatter-brained scientist, the nerd, etc. – but there is no logical proof that engineering would induce this type of behaviour.

The most likely explanation of this phenomenon will therefore be addressed in the sequel to this book. For the moment, we will content ourselves with the conclusion that statistically it is incredibly improbable that there does not exist a correlation between engineers and poor dress-sense, based purely on empirical data. For those who are still not convinced, please consider the following photos of 3 real engineers and one guy who actually knows how to dress – the difference is pretty shocking:

Figure 3.1 Three real engineers and some other guy

So, the net conclusion from Section 1 is that, by the time they enter the world outside university, engineers are significantly disadvantaged in terms of physical attractiveness. But, again, this is only the tip of the iceberg, as we shall see.

Section 2 - Engineers and Social Graces.

There is a fundamental difference between engineering courses at university and other courses. Most non-engineering courses consist primarily of bullshitting. Not that they are totally free of content, or that there isn't ever an occasional quantifiable measure of capability, but primarily students of arts, law, humanities, politics, social sciences, etc. learn how to make their meagre knowledge and feeble thoughts sound impressive. In some ways, this is the 20th century version of rhetoric (the study of argument without content, which in ancient Greece and modern Parliaments is used to make mindless ideas appear logical and convincing). But since the ancient Greeks, the primary tool has moved from rhetoric, which still allowed for intelligent discussion among intelligent people, to pure BS, in which language is used to actively hide the true idea being expressed in a mist of euphemism, obtuse or obscure observations and obfuscation. The objective being to say something that sounds impressive but which cannot be contradicted because even on careful analysis, it is impossible to work out exactly what you've actually said, and what you meant by it. In the hands of an expert, bullshitting is a true art form, and we in no way suggest that it is to be despised or reviled. What we do suggest is that engineers need to get better at it. Because engineers have the misfortune to study and work in an environment in which there is usually a correct answer, or where one solution can be tested against another and shown to be better or worse. And it is also an environment in which clarity is imperative and obfuscation will be penalised. In other words, an environment in which there are natural impediments to developing one's ability to bullshit.

To demonstrate the importance of this deficiency, let us move the scene to that most awful of events, a cocktail party – but one of many examples of a situation where social graces are key. Let us consider, without loss of generality, a situation in which one attractive[14] lady is surrounded by 4 men, of whom three are engineers and one is an Italian major. Each of the four would like to convince the lady to share her phone number with them. Let us listen to an excerpt from the conversation:

E1 ... but the thing is, you can then solve the linear equation in frequency space, and then when you take the inverse Fourier

---

[14] Hence obviously not an Engineer (Ed.)

transform, you discover that the flow field is actually very different from what Hegarty's analysis suggests. Isn't that fascinating?

L   *Indeed, fascinating.*

E2   *Does the level of turbulence still scale with the 1/3 power of the Reynolds Number?*

E1   *That's an interesting question ...*

E3   *I read a paper last Saturday which said that it was actually with the ¼ power in the case of irrotational flow ..*

L   *Fascinating. So what do you guys when you're not thinking about fluid mechanics?*

E2   *Actually, a lot of people thing that engineers only ever think about engineering. But that's not true at all.*

E1   *Yes, yesterday evening over a few beers, E3 and I spent hours talking about the implications of Bell's Inequality, even though there are no practical engineering applications of that work!!*

E2   *Well not yet, but maybe someday in the field of quantum computation or cryptography it will be useful.*

E1   *I don't really think it will though. As I was saying to E3 yesterday, for something to be of practical value, you really need to have not just statistically valid experimental data, but also a mathematically valid understanding of those data.*

E3   *But I'm firmly in the empiricist camp on this one.*

I   *I'm an Italian major.*

L   *So do you speak Italian. That's such a beautiful language.*

I   *Well, I'm actually fluent in Italian.*

L   *So, say something to me in Italian.*

I   *(thinks ....)   tu ha due buchi neri y denti bello e io trova che tu e' molto bello*

L   *Wow that sounds beautiful, what does it mean?*

I   *I just said that you have such beautiful dark eyes and a wonderful smile and you are very beautiful. It's actually a line from a poem called "Infinity" by Leonardo da Vinci, but it's perfect for you.*

L   *(blushes). It's so romantic. I'm always fascinated by the Renaissance.*

I   *The what?*

E2   *You know, I've heard that Leonardo started to develop some of the preliminary tools of calculus, even before Newton or Leibniz.*

E1   *But really, the most interesting aspects of Calculus came much later. I remember how fascinated I was the first time I realised that even a non-continuous function could be treated as piecewise differentiable and that the various derivatives of the Dirac delta function could be used to manage the discontinuities.*

.... (skipping 30 minutes of tedium, finally the Italian major, who has been silent, speaks:)

I   *I don't really follow all this. I flunked multiplication in junior high, and I haven't had to take any more math or science since then.*

L   *You mean you know nothing at all about math or science or engineering?*

I   *Nothing at all. I hate math.*

L   *That is the most romantic thing anyone has ever said to me. Please let me take you to my room and make passionate love to you all night long.*

I   *(to engineers) Hasta la vista baby. (to L) That's an Italian proverb from the Renaissance.*

L   *Please, talk more Italian to me ....*
      (L and I leave, arm-in-arm).

E1   *She wasn't very bright, was she?*

E2   *No.*

Section 3 - Engineers Interacting with Women.[15]

Over the past 30 years, our understanding of the human brain has been greatly improved. We're still at about the same level now as the ancient Greeks' understanding of nuclear physics, but nonetheless further than we were. And one of the first learnings is that, whatever political correctness might preach to us, male and female brains are not identical. There are important differences, most importantly in the desire to communicate – on average, the female communicates 3 times as much as the male – and in our ability to observe non-verbal signals, at which the female is significantly more adept.

These are then reinforced socially (again we repeat, we do not condone, encourage or condemn social practices, we just report them[16]). Boys play sports and learn to be aggressive, to compete, to win and lose, to be right and wrong, to glory in victory and accept defeat. Girls learn to get along,

---

[15] this is one of the few sections in which male and female engineers differ – the careful reader will see that the very characteristics which worsen the tragic situation of the male engineer may in fact help the female engineer in her interactions with men, giving her a slight advantage over her female rivals – an advantage which sadly is greatly overwhelmed by the many disadvantages cited elsewhere, and which is also rendered irrelevant in the many catastrophic cases in which two desperate souls, a male engineer and a female engineer, decide to settle for each other when all hope of a real relationship disappears.

[16] if you would like to change society, please contact Dr. J. Dorofi, PhD, who has similar plans.

and are discouraged from being overly competitive. You don't win a game of dolls – and if you do, your friends won't let you play next time.

The net effect of the physiological and societal factors is to lead to two pretty much incompatible species, women and men. A large part of the difference can be summed up in one simple phrase: men are goal-oriented, women are process-oriented. Men see and end-point and just want to get there. Women don't focus on the end-point, they see a process of getting there, and focus on that. So, when the woman comes to the man and says "what shoes should I wear?", the man has no hope of getting the answer right. Because she doesn't want a correct answer. She wants to communicate about shoes. And the man, of course, both doesn't understand this, and doesn't want to talk about shoes. So he says "the red ones", and he thinks, "problem solved" and goes back to watching football on tv. While of course the woman, having not had a good shoe discussion, will be back in two minutes, a bit more pissed off, trying to start a bracelet discussion, or a dress discussion.

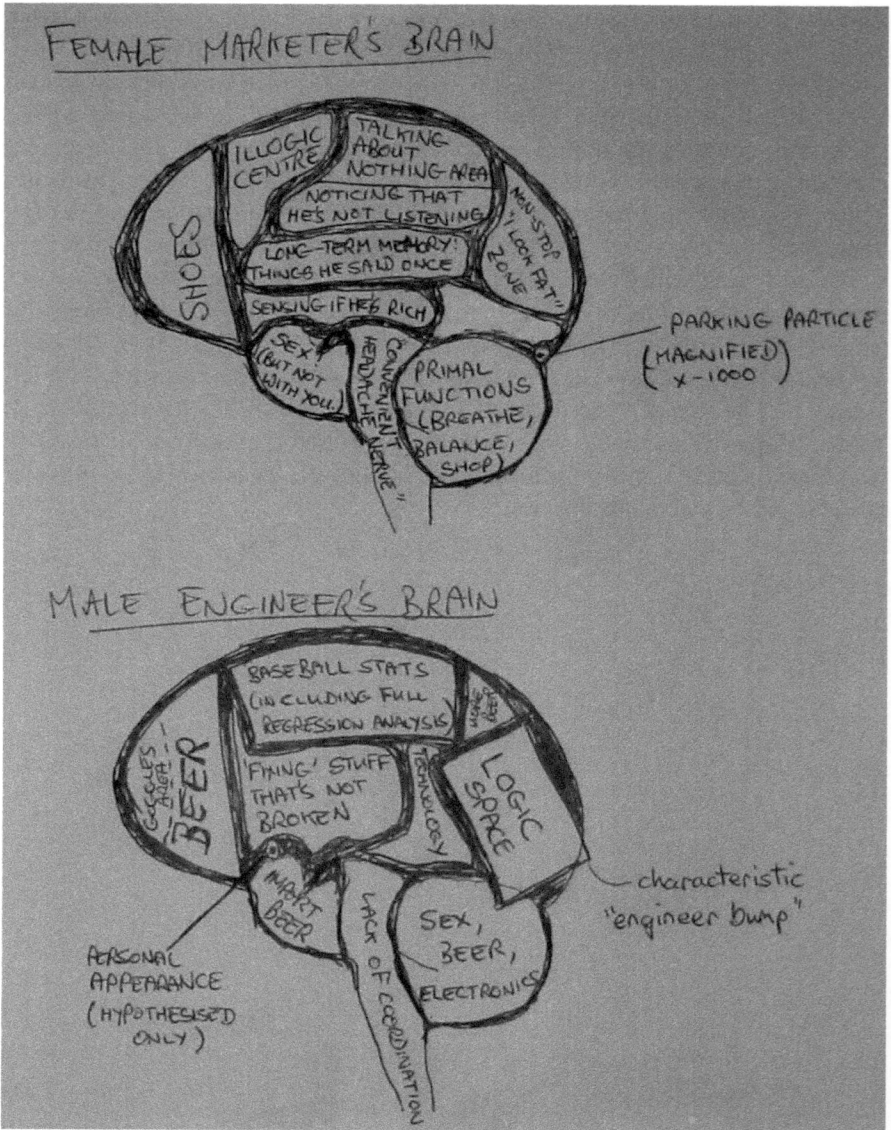

Figure 3.2 Brains of Female Marketer and Male Engineer
Using the latest brain-scanning technology, scientists at the Johns Hopkins University have begun to understand some of the fundamental reasons why male engineers do not interact well with non-engineering women. The above examples, considered "statistically representative" by the project team, show a comparison between the brains of a female marketer and a male engineer. The observations speak for themselves.

This may seem like an aside to the discussion on engineers. But think again. Think about the qualities that engineers have. The most important and valued quality (the superlative is a little bit excessive, since it's also the only quality), the thing that engineers do better than anyone else, is their ability to solve problems. And the greatest satisfaction for a typical engineer is to solve a problem. (remember, he doesn't have much else in life). So when faced with a dilemma like "which shoes should I wear", he immediately resolves the problem with a quick, clear and concise answer, 100% for efficiency, 0% for communication.

Compare this with, say, a lawyer being asked the same question. First, he will have to think about the problem, being a little slower than an engineer. Then he will be incapable, as lawyers are, of giving a concise answer, being used as he is to being paid by the word. His answer will almost certainly be wrong, but it will appear to his innocent mate as if at least he's made some effort to communicate.

Or consider the case of the Business graduate, who's just completed his MBA and is working at Burger King. He too will create a positive impression because he genuinely will not be able to answer the question. His slow brain reactions will take several seconds to register the concept of shoes, that they go on feet, he will no doubt have forgotten where they are going that evening, his thought process in getting from a question to an answer will have to be restarted, not having been used since he was 12, and to his delighted partner, his comments like "I'm not sure" will display an open-mindedness and an interest level which will be positively charming, while his questions like "where are we going?" will give the false impression that he's contemplating which footwear would be most appropriate for the particular occasion.

In short, the engineers' very strengths, limited as they are, will work against him, exactly as his weaknesses also work against him, in the key area of interactions with women. We will not investigate this very depressing conclusion any further at this point.

Section 4 - Engineers Interacting with Other People

Whether interacting with women or men, engineers suffer one further disadvantage. To the average engineer, other people who are not engineers appear stupid[17].

---

[17] There is an interesting corrolary to this – that most non-engineers think that most of the engineers they know are quite stupid too. We will not delve further into that at this stage in the book, but it may be elucidated in later chapters.

In you're not an engineer, and you're hearing this for the first time, please do not shoot the messenger. This is the reality. The engineer hears you worrying about problems that are easy to solve. He sees you focusing on details that are irrelevant. At work, he sees you preparing beautiful powerpoint charts to present the wrong solution, and then sees the VP believe you and not him on the basis of the charts. This only builds on the impression he had of you at university, for example in math classes you might have taken together (when he was a freshman and you were about to graduate), or in line at the supermarket when you struggled to figure out if you had enough change to pay.

There are two theories which explain this perception.

Explanation 1.
People who are not engineers are, for the most part, pretty dim.

Explanation 2.
Engineers are not necessarily the most perceptive people when it comes to appreciating qualities not directly related to solving technical problems.

There are compelling cases for and against each of these explanations, and rather than get involved in the debate, which is irrelevant to the objectives of this book, we will simply apply Ockham's Razor in a totally inappropriate manner and select the shorter explanation, thus explanation 1, as being the key reason. Since most of the readers of this book will be engineers, this fits best with their perceptions and will minimise critical feedback.

What is important, though, is how this perception influences engineers' interactions with other people, and in particular, how it interferes with the process whereby they might theoretically learn from experience and so improve themselves. We will look at some examples to explore this point.

Example 1.
Engineer Joe (we will not call him Tim because that might be considered libellous) sees a pretty lady in a gym and decides to talk to her. Now, while the dynamics of the situation are very clearly that it is he who desires the conversation and not she, nonetheless Joe's focus is not so much on helping her to enjoy the conversation, but rather on educating her. For example, on discovering that she hasn't quite grasped the subtleties of the application of the Laplace Transform to Process Control of a plug-flow reactor, he will sacrifice his time and explain it to her with

infinite patience, until she politely says that she now understands it but must leave, even if she's only been there for 10 minutes.[18]

Example 2

Joe meets the same lady again several months later, when her evasionary tactics momentarily fail. However, in a moment of uncalled-for generosity, she decides to help him. She explains to him some of the minor flaws in his approach to meeting women, which we won't enumerate here for want of space, and suggests some techniques to improve – for example, to try to talk about things that the woman might be interested in, to wear matching socks, and so on. Now another man would take these words of wisdom to heart, but for the engineer, these represent nothing but the wild ramblings of an inferior thinking being, who could not possibly understand things better than he does. As in the previous example, he contentedly ascribes their failure to "hit it off" as being due to her, and resolves to keep looking for someone worthy of him intellectually.

I think no further examples are needed here to predict where this approach is likely to lead in the long-term.

Section 5 - Engineers Interacting with Women II: "lack of practice phenomenon"

Most engineers (and this is NOT their fault, and certainly not their choice) have been in university classes which were 80% male, and then work in environments which are also very male dominated. Of the few females who share these locations, many are themselves engineers, while others have learned to live with and tolerate the ways of engineers. The result is that when you, a female, meet a typical engineer outside work or

---

[18] Laplace Transforms provide the basis for one of the nerdiest jokes in history, which is repeated here for completeness. During the papacy of Pope John-Paul II of Poland, he and 100 cardinals were flying back to Rome after a trip to New York for some Christmas shopping. Suddenly, half-way across the atlantic, the flight started jumping about wildly, as if beset by a terrible turbulence. The cardinals feared for their lives, as the pilot struggled without success to stabilize the aircraft. Some of the cardinals approached the pope and suggest that their only hope lies in requesting divine intervention. However, John Paul II scoffed at this idea, saying God has better things to do with His time. He gets up from his seat on the right hand side of the aisle and crosses over to a seat on the left hand side. Immediately the turbulence disappeared and they were again flying calmly towards Rome. One of the younger cardinals asked the pope if he's just witnessed a miracle, but the Holy Father replied that it was nothing of the sort, to regain stability all that had to be done was to move the dominant pole to the left half of the plane.

college, you might be the first non-engineer-adjusted woman he's met in the past 3 months.

Briefly, the consequences of even a brief interaction are likely to be disastrous to any chance the engineer might have imagined he had of ever sleeping with this female. Based on the analyses and examples given above, the proof of this conclusion is left as an exercise for the student. The proof should be purely theoretical in nature, and should not rely on empirical data in any way. In fact, for legal reasons, even empirical validation of the theoretical conclusion is strongly discouraged, at least until the engineer has studied the rest of this book.

Figure 3.3 Rather than end this chapter on a negative note, and just to prove it isn't physically impossible, above is a photo of an engineer with two beautiful women.

Chapter 4   A Self-Evaluation Quiz for Engineers

At this stage of the book, having highlighted some of the failings from which many engineers suffer, it is worth looking at yourself in a quantitative, scientific manner, to ascertain where exactly you personally stand. So we have designed a self-evaluation quiz.

This quiz isn't intended to totally demoralize you, though realistically that'll probably be the outcome. As you answer the questions, and particularly as you read the analysis that follows, try to remember that there are more important things in life than being able to interact with and attract members of the opposite sex.

I know this isn't easy for engineers, but for this exercise it's important that you answer the questions before looking at the interpretation, and that you answer spontaneously rather than doing a complex analysis of how you feel about a particular topic. There will be plenty of scope for independent analysis of the results, because while we give a topline simplistic interpretation below, we leave statistical, differential, stochastic, multivariable and any other analyses fully up to you. So, feel free to interpret the results as you see fit.

For example, one engineer who tried this test discovered that he scored statistically higher on prime-numbered questions, which led him to conclude that, rather than accept our damning conclusion, he just needed to focus his attention on ladies with strong prime number characteristics. Another was encouraged to see that while his answers were not good, and in fact appeared to get worse as the test went on, the second derivative of his results (d^2A/dn^2) was positive, suggesting that if the test had continued for another 71 questions, his final average score would have classified him as "quite likely to meet a woman one day".

So, for each of the following questions, please select one answer, a, b, c, or d. When you've completed all the questions, please see the interpretations which follow.

1. Walking out the door one morning you notice that you are wearing one brown shoe and one black shoe. What do you do?
    a. go back in and search for the other brown shoe.
    b. change to a pair of blue pants so they won't clash with either shoe.
    c. set up a 1-to-1 correspondence between shoes and socks, and devise an algorithm to choose an appropriately coloured sock for each and every shoe, for each n, starting from from $n = 1$ (left foot), and continuing until all feet are appropriately socked, realising that this process will only be practical for those with a finite number of feet but nonetheless attempting to find a theoretical generalisation to non-finite cases[19].
    d. Continue on. I'm not sure I see the problem here: two feet, two shoes – sounds about right.

2. While trekking through the Amazonian jungle with only a standard *TI55* calculator, you are set upon by a gang of Kalahari bushmen, who tell you that they will cut your tongue out unless you can tell them the formula for the mass of a 6-dimensional hypersphere of radius R and density given by the formula $\rho(r) = \rho_0(1-r/2R)$ in 5 minutes or less. How do you react?
    a. Calmly explain to them that this isn't the Kalahari and they have no more rights than you have to be there, and if they don't fuck off out of your way you'll beat them up with those moves you saw in the Karate kid movies.
    b. Aggressively question whether there is any physically meaningful interpretation of density in 6-dimensional space, which renders their question meaningless.[20]

---

[19] In the *Principia Mathematica*, Russell and Whitehead attempted to generalise the concept of sequential processes to non-finite numbers, with partial success, but to the best of the authors' knowledge, it hasn't been demonstrated that their approach can be applied to socks.

[20] Although the bushmen may be able to defend their point of view if they have read Russell's reflections on this topic, in which he concludes that many of the confusions of philosophy are resolved if we accept that we live in a 6-dimensional world "I came to the conclusion that what, in the space of physics, counts as a point, or more precisely, as a 'minimal region' is really a 3-dimensional complex of which the total of one man's percepts is an instance" (Russell, *My Philosophical Development*, Unwin Paperbacks, 1959, p 79). This is also possible if they are able to derive a viable string theory or M-theory in which the total number of assumed dimensions is 6, of which 3 are curled up at a microscopic level.

c. Pause for about 30 seconds as if thinking, then say "But that's obviously *16/9 π ρ_0^2 π R^7/L,* where L is the appropriate length-correction factor to account for the curvature of 6-dimensional spacetime in the presence of massive objects."

d. Sing a verse of Alice's Restaurant and hope they'll join in and you'll all be friends.

3. Thinking about the last time you were introduced to an attractive woman and wanted to ask her out, which of these best describes the progress you made?

   a. Was overcome by nerves and stood there mute looking like an idiot until she walked away looking unimpressed.

   b. While I was telling her about my latest project to impress her and I was just getting to the bit about how we've increased the energy efficiency by 13%, she turned and ran screaming out the door. I think she must have seen a spider or something.

   c. Spilt red wine on her white dress while demonstrating the interrelationship between surface tension and viscosity.

   d. She gave me her phone-number and asked me to call her. She told me not to worry if her mother, who didn't speak English, answered, just to try again later. I tried several times, but her mother always answered, and I never could understand what she was saying. (When I got my next phonebill, there were $362 of charges for calls to China that I'm sure I didn't make).

4. After years of trying, you've finally persuaded that beautiful woman from Marketing to go home with you after the Christmas Party. In the taxi on the way home, she casually mentions that it's a pity the whole of the US didn't follow the example of Ohio and adopt that great idea of simply defining $\pi = 4$ in all of the US, as one of her staff told her that with $\pi = 4$ she could fit more bottles of ketchup in each container and so reduce transportation costs by 30%. How to you respond?

   a. "As soon as we get to my apartment, I'll program my computer to give you a graphical demonstration of why this isn't realistic. The sex will have to wait until next year."

   b. "An interesting idea … however, the danger would be that in some states they might decide that it would be better to define $\pi = 3$, and in those states then, your transport costs would go *up*. I don't think it's worth the risk."

   c. "What's stopping your from using it anyway? For Marketing purposes, $\pi = 4$ is probably going to be one of the most realistic assumptions going into your sales forecast."

   d. "Did I ever tell you that I'm able to recite π to 1000 decimal places. When I was in high school, I learnt another 20 digits every Saturday night when all the other kids were wasting time dancing and drinking and stuff. Listen, and see if you spot any mistakes: three-point-one-four-one-five-nine-two-six- ...."[21]

5. Your 83-year-old grandmother asks your opinion on what colour shoes she should wear to your cousin's wedding. What colour do you suggest?
   a. Blue
   b. Blue
   c. Brown
   d. Magenta

---

[21] At the time of Russell's death, the decimal expansion of π which had been worked out did not contain 3 consecutive 7's, and it was not known if further expansion would eventually show three consecutive 7's or not . This led to a very heated debate between Russell and Brouwer on the topic of whether it was valid to deny the law of the excluded middle in the case of propositions which it was neither possible to prove true or to prove false. This may not appear relevant to this book at first glance, but in fact it is. To take an obvious example, imagine that an engineer asks a lady if she would like to sleep with him, and she replies "I will sleep with you IF there are three consecutive 7's in the decimal expansion of π, AND I will sleep with you if there are NOT three consecutive 7's in the decimal expansion of π". In this case, Brouwer's position would have been that, since it is not possible to decide if there are three consecutive 7's or not, the proposition is neither true or false, and therefore the lady would NOT have to sleep with the engineer. Russell, apparently aware of and sympathetic to the implications for engineers' sex-lives, did not agree, and believed it was "preposterous" to say that just because it wasn't verifiable, it was neither true nor false. Readers interested in a more detailed exposition of this point are referred to Russell's *Inquiry into Meaning and Truth.*
However, lest the matter be considered trivial and Brouwer's objection ridiculous, consider the equally likely possibility of two identical twin sisters being approached by an engineer. The first replies "I will sleep with you only IF there are three consecutive 7's in the decimal expansion of π", while the second replies "I will sleep with you only if there are NOT three consecutive 7's in the decimal expansion of π". By Russell's logic, it would appear that the engineer, indifferent to which sister sleeps with him, is onto a sure thing. However, in reality, it will not be possible for the engineer to prove to either sister that *she* in fact should sleep with him, only that either she or her sister should – and of course, it is not reasonable to expect either sister to sleep with him without verification that it is indeed she, and not her sister, who should do so. This suggests that Brouwer may have a point. The authors have not found any proposed solutions to this question in the recent philosophical literature, and have had their paper suggesting a threesome as the only logically acceptable answer rejected by the *Journal of Philosophical Investigations of Manila.* The matter remains under debate.

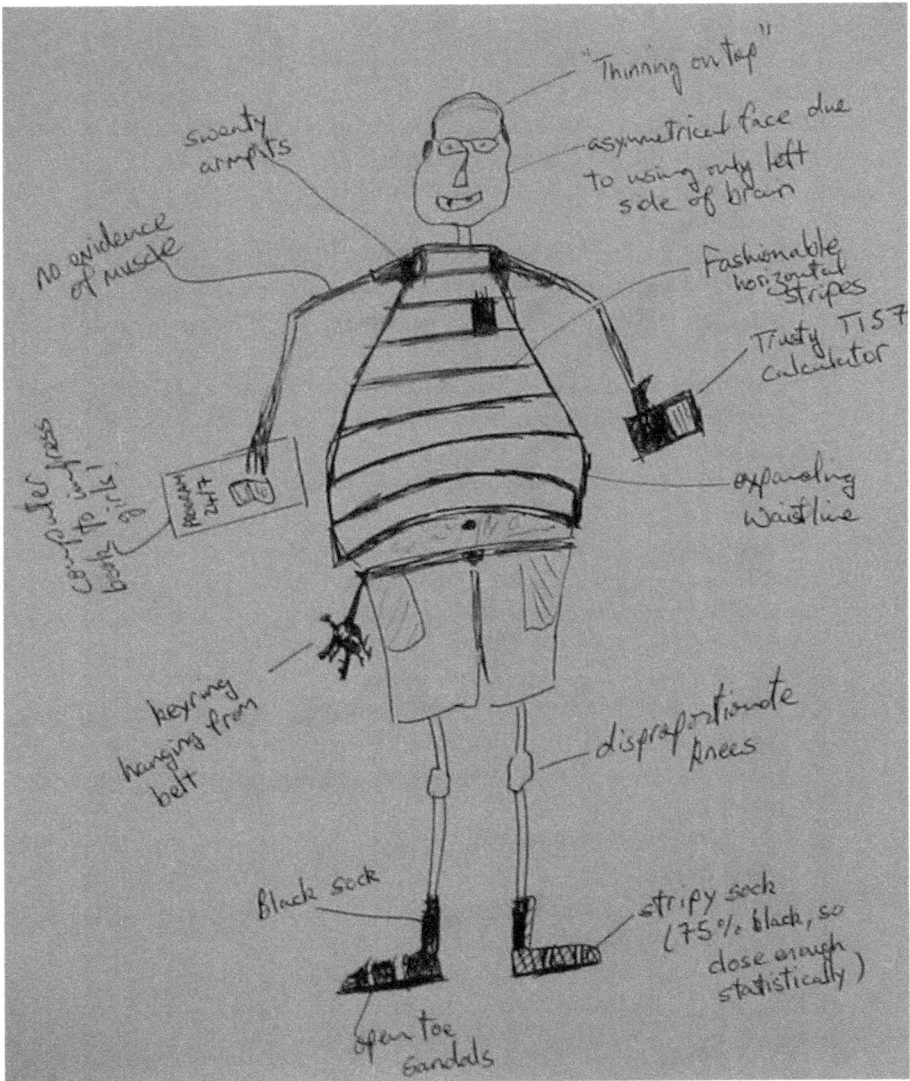

Figure 4."Engineer on the hunt", the classic 1993 portrait of an unidentified undergratuate senior engineer entering the Student Bar of the University of North Carolina, hoping to meet a woman. We do have the technology to include also a simulation of his impact on the aroma surrounding him, but for obvious reasons we didn't, and we hope you'll appreciate this.

6. You decide that to increase your chances of succeeding with the woman of your dreams, you are going to start working out every day. After 1 month of working out, the woman invites you to a Barry Manilow concert the following Tuesday. How do your reply?
   a. "Sure. Oh, no, wait, sorry, I can't make it. Tuesday I've got to go to work out."
   b. "I appreciate the thought, but I don't like Barry Manilow. If ever you get tickets for Metallica or something, let me know. Why not ask Bob from Accounting, most guys in Finance like Barry Manilow."
   c. "I don't think so. I think you're only after me for my body now that I'm going to the gym every day. I would only consider dating someone who respects me as a person."
   d. "Sure. Should I bring the condoms or will you?"

7. You are playing a round of golf at St. Andrews with Jack Nicklaus, Henry Kissenger and Christy Turlington. On the 13th hole, your ball comes to rest 6 inches behind a sprinkler-head just to the right of the green. How do you proceed?
   a. Chip the ball over the sprinkler head.
   b. Consult the rules of golf book in your bag, explain to your playing partners that you're taking relief from an immovable object, and move the ball one foot to the right of the sprinkler head, not nearer the hole.
   c. Putt the ball to the right of the sprinkler head, using the slope of the green to bring the ball down towards the hole.
   d. Lift and drop the ball further back behind the sprinkler-head, within two club-lengths of where it came to rest.

8. Which of the following proverbs best sums up your philosophy of relationships:
   a. If wishes were horses, beggars could ride.
   b. A bird in the hand is worth two in the bush.
   c. Never look a gift-horse in the mouth.
   d. He who goes to bed with a dog wakes up with fleas.[22]

9. You are a walking down a sidestreet in Rome drinking a strongly fermented beverage when suddenly a genie appears out of the bottle,

---

[22] Irish proverb: *An té a luíos leis an madaí, éireóidh leis na dreancaidí* … it is not known if Russell was aware of this prior to writing his introduction to Wittgenstein's *Tractatus*, some of which he later retracted..

and says you can make any three wishes you like, and then she will randomly grant one of them. However, she says this in French, and you don't understand what she's saying. What do you do?

a. Go back to the shop and buy another 10 bottles of the stuff to bring back home.

b. Finally realise that you should have taken French instead of physics in high-school.

c. Gather a crowd around you by claiming loudly that you've just worked another miracle, then with them as witnesses, quickly run to the Vatican[23] and ask the Pope to canonise you. Should he refuse, set up a new religion with your new followers, keeping in mind that "only the true Messiah denies his divinity".

d. Ask her to repeat the question in Italian, since you're in Rome. Then realise that didn't really help since you don't understand Italian either.

10. After 3 months living together with your current girlfriend, she comes into the room in a very sexy negligee, curls up on your knee and whispers gently in your ear that in her three months with you she has never had an orgasm, and would like to change that. How do your respond?

a. Reassure her that it is a problem that many women have, and that as the understanding man that you are, there is no way you would use this as a reason to break up with her.

b. Tell her that in your religion it's considered inappropriate to actually enjoy sex, especially before marriage, and that therefore you have been consciously trying not to get her to an immoral level of passion.

c. Tell her that there's 6 innings to go in the Cubs game, and that you'd really rather if she'd put on some clothes and go out and buy you some beers.

d. Try sleeping with her.

See details of how to calculate your score on the next page.

---

[23] In his indespensible *Guia turistica Romana*, Russell suggests taking the metro A to the last stop, Ottaviano, would be quicker, although Wittgenstein points out that this depends on the location in space and time from which the proposition is made, and suggests that only a pictorial representation of the situation can determine if it is true.

<u>Scoring.</u>

#	a	b	c	d	Notes and Observations
1	0	5	10	5	Answer *c* is the best because almost certainly it means you will not make it to the office at all, and no quality of yours is more appreciated by your female colleagues than your absence.
2	10	7	3	0	Any strategy which results in your having your tongue cut out, so rendering you unable to speak, is going to greatly enhance your appeal to most women. You might think that this would be an obstacle in the area of oral sex, but trust me, that's not something that women will be thinking about when they meet an engineer.
3	3	0	7	10	Getting a phone number is always a start, and statistically there's always a chance that it might belong to an attractive woman. However, in general be suspicious if there is a country code or just a lot more numbers than usual.
4	5	10	8	0	But if you do ever meet a woman who might be impressed by your being able to recite π to 1000 decimal places, remember you can just bluff, it's not like she's going to know … alternatively, you can derive it on the spot using an appropriate Taylor's series expansion.
5	0	0	0	0	Never ever answer a woman's question about clothing with a simple, practical, helpful answer!! Ask her what dress she'll be wearing. What will the weather be like. What will the bridesmaids be wearing. Will there be fish or meat .. you don't need to understand how these are possibly relevant, just pretend that questions like this are matters of great importance to be evaluated carefully from every angle.
6	0	5	10	2	The strategy outlined in the answer a to this question has become known in academia as the Laska phenomenon.

7	10	0	8	2	In his 1968 classic *"Golf as an Aphrodisiac"*, Dr. Roger Alpeter, M.D., of Imperial College London, demonstrated that while there is nothing less attractive to women than an engineer *per se*, it is still possible for him to lower his attraction further by regularly discussing the intricacies of the rules of golf. This result was for a time wrongly believed by physicists to suggest that by a parallel process, it might be possible to reach temperatures below 0 Kelvin.
8	5	3	5	0	We apologise for this question. However, if there is one thing you need to remember, it is that women like dogs. And as a general rule, you should treat with great suspicion any woman who doesn't like dogs. So, mentioning any alleged negative characterisitc of dogs is not going to enamour any woman of you, except maybe one whom you would be better off without.
9	10	10	10	10	Some morale boosting bonus points just for being drunk in Rome instead of being stuck in front of a computer somewhere. At least now you know you won't end up with 0 points.
10	7	3	0	10	This is a notoriously tough question. Women in general are very difficult to understand, and frequently instead of saying something directly, they will make subtle hints, far to subtle for even many non-engineers to understand. Yet, impossible as it seems, with careful analysis it is occasionally possible to estimate what she might be trying to suggest. And if there's any possibility that what she might be suggesting is sex, then you have very little to lose by assuming that to be the case until she tells you differently.

Add up your points to get your total score: _____

Interpretation of your Score

Your score: **86-100**.
Grade: **A**. (well done!).
Interpretation. Our analysis suggests that, among engineers, you may have a slightly higher than average capacity to not provoke spontaneous regurgitation of dinner with your every comment. The scientific basis for this conclusion is very straightforward – in attaining a score above 85, you have demonstrated either a serious case of innumeracy or a willingness to lie and cheat, and either or both of these traits will make it much easier for you to talk to and interact with non-engineers, and particularly with non-engineer women.

Your score: **65-85**.
Grade: **B**.
Interpretation. This score puts you among the highest scoring of those who have accurately followed our guidelines for totaling up their scores. However, let's be realistic here, all through school you probably did really well in tests and exams, and did that ever help get your laid?? Unfortunately there's no reason to believe that this will be any different.

Your score: **45-64**.
Grade: **C**.
Interpretation. You might be tempted to see this result as saying that you are one of the most dull, average and mediocre members of a group of people who are already reviled throughout society for their dullness and mediocrity. However, this interpretation is probably over-optimistic, and any delusions of mediocrity you may harbour should be tempered by the reality that you are still an engineer.

Your score: **25-44**.
Grade: **D**.
Interpretation. In recent years there has been a significant drop off in religions vocations, making entry significantly less competitive. Have you considered this option?

Your score: **0-24**.
Grade: **F**.
Interpretation. . I don't think you need to look at this too negatively. While your every answer above reveals you to be the type of engineer whose inability to attract women is surpassed only by the strong

shuddering repulsion that women feel the moment you enter a room, which has been tested experimentally[24] and proved to work in less than 75 microseconds, even when the woman is not facing the door or is blindfolded[25] or otherwise sensually deprived, you probably knew this already and had adjusted to it.

---

[24] For example, refer to the paper by Russell's cousin, Benjamin Russell: "The Psychodiuretic Laska Effect", *JScPhA*, 11, 1993, pp 200-235.

[25] It is thought that this effect may allow physicists to choose between string theory and loop-quantum theory in their search for the ultimate understanding of quantum gravity. There is obviously a form of "information" passing from the engineer to the woman, although it is not clear which subatomic particles are involved. Should these prove to be massive, it should be possible, by modifying the repulsiveness of the engineer, the size of the room and the number of ladies present, to detect the variations these particles could provoke in the structure of space-time itself, and so, among other things, help us understand whether space and time are truly discrete at the planck scale. Those of you who have scored below 15 on this test could potentially find lucrative employment in this field, once the theoretical details have been worked out and the appropriate particle detectors designed.

The implications implicit in this for Russell's theroy of undecidable propositions are pretty evident (do you get to sleep with the twin who says she will if string theory is true or the one who says she will if loop-quantum theory is true? etc.), and need not be discussed further here.

Chapter 5   Why It's Good to be an Engineer

After that quiz, it's probably time to improve morale a little, so in this chapter we've decided to put together some material that will show you why it's good to be an engineer.

- Ten qualities of engineers which make them attractive in the eyes of women:

  1. can calculate things
  2. not always obese
  3. dependable source of income
  4. ..
  5. ..
  6. ..
  7. ..
  8. ..
  9. ..
  10. ... (some research is ongoing to identify the final 7 traits ... we'll fill these in ~~before the book is published~~ in the sequel).

- Famous Engineers throughout History who were successful with women:

  1. the guy who build all those ships, probably must have had some success

2. there must be more ...
3. was Bill Gates an engineer? With all that money, he can't have done all that badly.
4. ..
5.
6.
7.
8.
9.
10.

- Social success and meeting women isn't everything anyhow. OK, so non-engineers may get laid more often, but ...

    1. most of them don't even know the difference between fugacity and enthalpy, even though they're even measured in different units !
    2. some of them are still using Windows 2000.
    3. many of them drive cars with clearly sub-optimal fuel-efficiency.
    4. engineers usually beat them in important machine-code programming competitions
    5.
    6. ..

OK, perhaps this wasn't quite as good for morale as we had assumed ... let's move onto the next section which will give more practical tips.

Section C: Dating Analytics

Better Living Through Equations

Chapter 6   The Dating Success Probability Model

Those of you who opened the contents page and didn't immediately turn to the chapters on sex looking for nude pictures probably turned first to this section, from whose title it might appear that it would contain information of immediate practical use in increasing your chances of getting laid this year. Of course, we too hope that it will help, but suggest that hopes remain realistic ...

In many respects, many everyday phenomena can be described by an equation, and it is our firm belief that dating is no exception. There is some debate on whether a first principles approach to dating is possible but it is clear than an analytical approach of some kind can be useful in optimizing your personal situation.

The chapter comprises two sections. In the first, we outline a very simple but representative model of how one should think about dating in a world where, realistically, most people are going to react with something between laugher and disgust to any romantic approach you might make to them.

In the second, we look briefly at the practical steps you may take to address this, and direct you to the appropriate sections.

Theoretical Dating Model.

The concept here is very straightforward. You may know people who walk into a room or a bar, choose the person they would most like to spend the evening/night with, and have a reasonable probability of succeeding in that objective. If you were one of them, you would not have bought this book. For the rest of us, instead of focusing too much on one specific target (although that situation is covered in the chapter on competitive dating), we need to consider the world of dating in probabilistic terms. If over a period of 1 year, for example, we make n approaches to women, and if the probability of "success", which might be defined, for example, as getting a phone number, or more optimistically of getting *her* phone number, of each attempt i is p_i, and if we make the assumption that q_i is the probability of eventually starting a relationship with woman i if she gives you her phone number, then it is evident that the probability of having at least one relationship within the year is given by

$$P_R \quad = \quad (1 - \Pi_1^n [1 - p_i q_i])$$

where the symbol Π_1^n means that you multiply the n terms in square brackets together, each time using a different value of i, from *1* to *n*.

{In case the logic here is not obvious, think of it this way. If p_i is the probability that you get the phone number of woman i, and q_i is the probability that you start a relationship with her *if* you get her phone-number, than clearly $p_i q_i$ represents the probability that you start a relationship with woman i. Then *[1 - $p_i q_i$]* is simply the possibility that, for whatever reason, you do *not* start a relationship with woman i.

If we then consider the analogous situation for woman j, the probability that you do not start a relationship with her either is *[1 - $p_j q_j$]* . And so the probability that you do not start a relationship with either woman i or woman j is the multiple of these two terms: *[1 - $p_i q_i$].[1 - $p_j q_j$]*. If you talk to n women, then the probability that you will not start a relationship with any of them is clearly given by $\Pi_1^n [1 - p_i q_i]$, and 1 minus this quality is the probability that you *do* start a relationship with at least one of them.}

If we assume that your objective is to have a relationship, that is to maximise P_R, then the following observations are relevant.

- Each term *[1 - $p_i q_i$]* is less than or equal to 1. Whenever this term is less than one, it means (as is obvious) that by talking to her, you are increasing that chances that you will have a relationship. So, as n increases, so P_R increases.
- The larger the two probabilities p_i and q_i are, the more different the term is from 1, and so the more it increases your likelihood of having a relationship. Again this is pretty obvious, but it's reassuring for an engineer to know he's on solid mathematical ground.

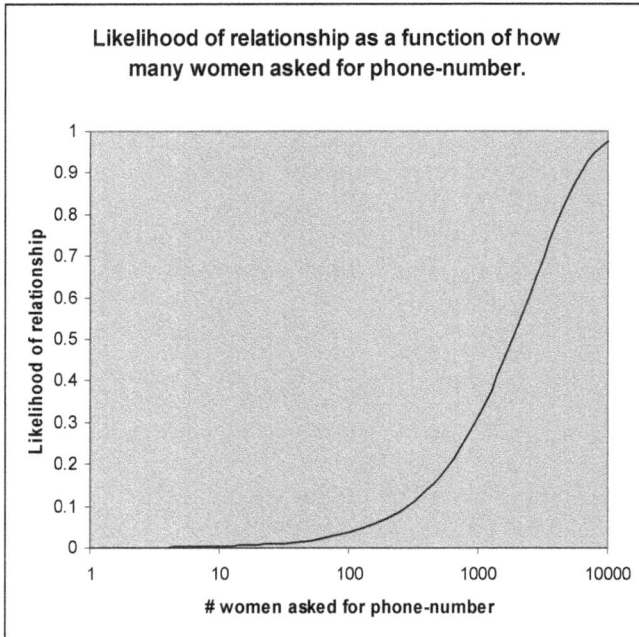

Figure 6.1 The graph shows how, independently of any other improvements, simply increasing the number of people you ask out, provided each invitation is linearly independent of the others (e.g. not someone who knows them!) can increase your chance of having a relationship. The above data consider the following data, gathered from a study of 573 Engineers' in a various singles groups by Walker and Jackson (*JPhRZ*, 2, 2001, pp21-37). In this over-simplified example, the "averages" are assumed as constants for all cases:

- Probability that a typical woman, when asked by an Engineer, will give him a phone-number = 0.14
- Probability that the number she gives him has more than 75% of digits in common with her actual number = 0.23
- Probability that engineer will have nerve to call her & ask her out = 0.24 (some alcohol may be involved)
- Probability that she will agree to go out with him, and not stand him up = 0.15 (includes sympathy dates)
- Probability that the date will lead to a relationship (precise definition was not specified in survey) = 0.31

As the graph shows, an engineer who asks fewer than 10 women for their phone numbers has a negligible chance of a relationship in any given year, while an engineer who asks 1000 women has a 31% chance of at least one relationship.

Putting these into practical terms:

- The first point above implies that you should never reject an opportunity to talk to a woman just because it has a low probability of success, provided it has a non-zero probability of success.[26] And given the well documented and experimentally verified total incomprehensibility and unpredictability of women, it is highly unlikely that you, an engineer, will ever be in a position to be absolutely sure that the probability is zero. For example, that stunning blonde in the fruit-and-vegetable aisle might just have fought with her boyfriend and dumped him, and might now be determined to show up at the party tonight with the least physically attractive man in the city just to have the pleasure of telling her now ex. "at least, he's better than you!" In which case, you will probably perfectly fit the bill, and the only thing you need to work on would be to convince her how much more powerful the statement would be if she could say truthfully "and he's better than you in bed as well!"[27]
  In the scientific literature, maximising n would be referred to as an "increased sampling rate strategy."

---

[26] There are two caveats to this. The first is that the calculation above assumes that the n women are linearly independent, that is, that the probability p_i of success with woman i is not in any way affected by any interactions with woman j, and vice versa. Obviously this will not be valid if, for example, you ask out a woman, and, having been rejected, ask out her sister who was standing next to her the whole time. In such cases, you really need to analyse whether it might be best to select the one most promising case and approach that woman only. That said, having been rejected by the first woman, if you believe there is still a non-zero possibility with another, even her sister, then go for it!

The second caveat, and it applies particularly strongly to examples like those mentioned in the previous paragraph of this footnote, can be summed up by a conversation overheard in an Engineering drawing room: "She doesn't seem interested, but sure I'll ask her out anyway. What have I got to lose?" "Nothing at all, ... except your dignity." In other words, there may come a point where, in your personal estimation, the shame and indignity of trying to hit on every woman you see will outweigh the slight increase in the success probability that this will bring. As to the location of this point, unfortunately, you will need to decide for yourself, as no general theory exists as yet to define precisely what level of indignity an engineer can sink to.

Rather than end this footnote here, the authors would like to point out to any women who suddenly find themselves being asked out by engineers left right and centre that we are neither proposing or opposing this – we are simply pointing out the inferences from the laws of probability and statistics, from which each individual engineer can then choose to proceed as he chooses, and for whose subsequent behaviour the authors hold no legal or moral responsibility whatsoever.

[27] This example was unfortunately chosen, in that we believe the probability of this occurring is exactly 0.

- The second point implies that you need both to improve your charm, wit and appearance when you approach women, and to improve your charm, wit, appearance, dating techniques, choice of restaurants, and so forth if she gives you her phone number. There are thousands of books out there already on how to do this. Most of these would fall under the general principle of increasing one's native attractiveness, a process which is not generally considered appropriate for a purely mathematical analysis. So we do not treat that in depth here. However, throughout this book there are some helpful suggestions. Indeed, we would however suggest that particular attention be paid, if it has not already been paid, to the chapter on Market Research Techniques, and particularly to the concept of targeting the right women and effectively selling yourself. This is the surest way to increase both p_i and q_i.

   In the literature, approaches like this would be referred to as "increased success rate strategies".

In summary, in this chapter we've demonstrated that by increasing the number of women you talk to, and/or by increasing your likelihood of succeeding with each of them, you maximise your chances of ending up in a relationship. A truly groundbreaking conclusion!

From an engineering perspective, the mathematics are quite simple, nearly trivial. So it should be of some comfort to the average engineer that the seemingly intractable problem of dating can be so simply represented. The next two chapters will tell you how to go about optimizing those key inputs, your "N" and your attractiveness.

Chapter 7   Why N Matters, and How to Increase Yours

You may just think of N as the first letter in the names Nuala, Norbert and Pneumonia, but in statistics, "n" is the number of cases, the sample space, for a particular situation. Which brings great possibilities for even the most desperate of situations as n gets large.

Take the example of Ken Griffey Jr, generally acknowledged to be a great ball player; he hits a bunch of home runs, makes a billion dollars or so a year and is probably quite popular with children. However, the dark side of Ken Griffey Jr. is that if you look at the percentage of home runs that he takes per at bat it's only about a miserable 5%. Really, only 5%!! And if you calculate on a per pitch basis, it is less than 1% !! And to think that he is regarded as one of the best players in the game today - what a chump !

So why is it that Ken Griffey Jr. is so successful? How can someone make so much money for doing something at which he succeeds less than 5% of the time??? It is because he doesn't just face one pitch. He doesn't just take one at-bat. He takes a *lot*. And there lies the key. Take a lot of at bats, increase the n, fight against your low success rate in a single event by making sure that there are a LOT of events.

In other words you need to get off your butt and start sampling.

How do you increase your N?
This is generally where most of your average "How to Meet Girls" type books start, and there are plenty of references to go off of (see for example "Meeting Girls" by Franz Kafka, "Eins, Zwei, Drei Mädchen" by Wolfgang von Goethe, or "The Old Man and the young - but legal - Girls" by Ernest Hemingway).

The gist of all of these works is that women are everywhere. Okay, maybe not in the engineering library, or in your engineering classes, or in the computer lab, but they are out there. Importantly, it has been scientifically shown that roughly 50% of the population is women, which amounts to a few BILLION ! Okay, if we take out those under 20, those above 40 (excluding the occasional Mrs. Robinson), the nuns, the lesbians (this is always a bummer), it is still over a billion.

On average, then, if we take a billion women, and divide that by the land surface area[28] (excluding the mermaids and women sailors, who are often nuns or lesbians anyways), we get a figure which is an amazing 20 women per square mile. Obviously, the women are not evenly distributed over this surface area, for example South Dakota has less than 3 women per square mile, though with all the livestock, the guys there aren't too lonely. So the summary point is that there are a lot of women out there.

Let's now take stock of your current N.

Each qualified sample requires asking a woman out to an event with romantic intent. All three elements have to be there for it to count. For example, asking a woman to pass the salt, no matter how alluringly stated, does not count. Likewise not counting is going with a woman to a movie, if it is not someone you would consider sleeping with (e.g. nun, relative, woman married to Navy Seal). Also, it doesn't matter what the woman thinks[29], it is only whether YOU have romantic intent. Finally, of course, it doesn't matter at all what the outcome of the request was (ranging from an evening of wild sex to disparaging laughter and public ridicule).

The time frame is the last 12 months. So start counting.

Done ? Enter the value here _____

If the number you entered is less than 10, then we have some work to do. Even with time off for Christmas and Columbus Day, you should be averaging at least one attempt per month, probably more like three.

The reason goes back to the average probability of success we outlined above. Based on our scientific work (we are both Ph.D.'s by the way), the mean performance of the median engineer is approximately 3 sigma from the female target. Even with the one sigma improvement due to the items listed above, your average chances are still only 2.27%. Now, we believe that everyone should have at minimum a 50% chance of having sex at

---

[28] Just very slightly less than 58 million square miles.
[29] This statement refers only to the statistical context of determining N, obviously. Do not take this out of context. At certain points of the dating ritual, what the woman thinks is actually quite important!

least once every year (which we are actively trying to make a part of the new UN Resolution on Human Rights). But will this be true for you if you're only having 10 dates per year? Let's use the Poisson distribution to make the calculation.

The Poisson distribution is derived from the formula

$$p_X(k) = exp(-\mu)\mu^k /k!$$

meaning that the probability of exactly k occurrences of an event X is given by the above formula, where $\mu = s\,\lambda$ represents the product of the frequency of attempts, s (in this case $s = 10/year$) and the probability that any individual attempt will be successful, λ (in this case $\lambda = 0.0227$). Substituting these values into the equation gives:

$$p(0) = 0.7969$$
$$p(1) = 0.1809$$
$$p(2) = 0.0205$$
$$p(3) = 0.0016$$
$$p(4+) = 0.00015$$

The Poisson distribution assumes independent events, in this case, for example, the women cannot talk to each other and say what a loser you are. It also assumes rare events, which generally should hold for engineers getting laid. Finally Poisson also assumes that there is no improvement in your chances as more experience builds, in other words, you make the same stupid mistakes over and over, which is also probably true.

So anyway, the math speaks for itself. At your current rate, even if you ask out 10 women on dates in a given year, you have an 80% chance of not getting laid even once[30]. It is really time for you to get to work. Now, what the above analysis clearly highlights is that, unless you are some kind of superbeing capable of creating a universe in which the base of natural logarithms will be different from 2.71828 ... , your best chances of improving your odds are to work on increasing $\mu = s\,\lambda$, namely either ask

---

[30] Of course, in calculating $p(0)$, a simpler approach is to simply consider the probability of failure (= 1-0.0227 = 0.9773) on each occasion and raise it to the power of the number of attempts. For 10 attempts, $(0.9773)^{10} = 0.7948$. That this number is not identical to 0.7969 is due to the fact that the Poisson distribution is an approximation which is strictly speaking exact only for an infinite number of trials. However, if you feel that your morale needs a boost, it is encouraging to note that reality is not as bad as the Poisson distribution suggests – indeed, as these numbers show, your chances of getting laid at least once in a given year are actually 0.21% higher than the Poisson distribution suggests. Theorists have suggested that Poisson was even less successful than typical engineers due to his fishy odor. [we apoligize for that – Ed.]

more people out, or have a higher success probability with each one. To have a 50% chance of getting laid in a given year, you'd typically want to have this product equal to about 0.7.[31]

(Again, careful readers will notice that we've conveniently assumed, as highlighted in a footnote above, that once the woman finds the engineer sufficiently attractive (prob assumed = 0.0227), then she will necessarily sleep with him – of course this is not true. Strictly speaking therefore, the 50% chance referred to here actually refers to having a 50% chance of going on a date with a woman who has not immediately decided not to sleep with you the moment she set eyes on you. However, the central message does not change.)

The main thing that most engineers fail to grasp is that to identify new potential women to ask out, and to arrange and survive dates requires work. Just as it takes time and effort to work through a thermodynamics problem set, design a new circuit or troubleshoot an operating system, it takes time and effort to date. However, while the work mightn't be as much fun, the rewards are generally much more interesting, except for those really cool problems where you derive something from first principles, like the Clausius Clapeyron equation from the equations of state,.

As with any engineering problem, it is going to take logic and execution.

Analysis of the Female Species
Our cumulative 50 odd years of careful observation of females has revealed several interesting features of their lifestyle. What is interesting, of course is to understand the activities and behavioral patterns of women. Just as Jacques Cousteau or Jane Goodall, planned their forays into the natural habitat of their target of interest, so must you understand and plan your encounters with women.

Fortunately for you, the heavy lifting has been done by us, and we can offer the following breakdown of activities, based on a 24 hour day (obviously there are large variations depending on day of the week):

---

[31] This is an interesting example of the inexactitude of the Poisson distribution for small sample sizes. Obviously, if you have only one date, but a 50% chance of success, they you'd have a value of $\mu = 0.5$ and still have a 50% chance ... but as we're dealing with engineers here, we didn't consider probabilities of this order of magnitude to be realistic. And anyhow, we're not too worried about people making angry complaints about getting laid more than we predicted they would.

Sleeping	7
Working	6
"Getting ready"	2.5
Eating	2
Fixing hair	1.5
Entertainment(bars, movies)	1
Shopping	1
Driving/Commuting	1
Talking on telephone	1
Exercising	0.5
Going to bathroom	0.5

These figures are for the average single woman in the U.S. For married women, the time distribution is quite different as approximately 3 hours per day is spent complaining about their husbands.

So when is the optimal time to strike? Again, we can do a simple analysis with what we term "accessibility factor" or AF. The AF term indicates how likely it will be that a woman will talk to you while performing a certain activity, and not call the police. For example, if you approach a woman while she is sleeping, especially if you come in through the window or make a phone call late at night, her willingness to go on a date will likely be low.

So we add a column for AF and multiply and sort accordingly. We have estimated the values for AF – in reality these will vary from person to person and you might want to revise these numbers to work out your own numbers. The scale is clearly relative. If for example you are a world-renowned expert on cheese, you may find it slightly easier to approach a woman while eating with a credible line. Similarly, the AF for women at work as it refers to you will obviously depend on how closely you work with them. While this can be a good area if the women, say, works in a different department of a large company that you work for, at approach at work can be less productive if the woman is, for example, a nun. The column on the right shows where you should be focusing:

Activity	Time	AF	Potential
Working	6	2	12
Eating	2	2.5	5
Entertainment(bars, movies)	1	5	5
Exercising	0.5	9	4.5
Shopping	1	4	4
Driving/Commuting	1	1	1
Sleeping	7	0.1	0.7
Fixing hair	1.5	0.2	0.3
"Getting ready"	2.5	0.1	0.25
Talking on telephone	1	0.1	0.1
Going to bathroom	0.5	0.1	0.05

With this information and analysis at hand, it is now time to actually approach women at the opportune moments and ask them out. However, this chapter offers no further guidance on how to do this successfully.

A few comments

Although it can be fraught with danger, approaching a woman at the place you work is often very effective. As the previous example pointed out, the competition is known and easy to evaluate, and there are many opportunities to observe the person of interest over time. Risks are also present, particularly if you work in government (e.g. are the President) or if things end or start badly.

Approaching women while they are eating is also a fairly good strategy. Generally, women are distracted while eating and are also in a good mood. So this is a good time to try.

The traditional notion of meeting women at bars works generally only during Spring Break or Mardi Gras, when large amounts of alcohol are being consumed. Generally, women are too concerned trying to look good to be bothered by actually having someone approach them. However, it is worth a try, especially as it can be used as an excuse to drink beer.

In the above chart we suggest that the highest potential for meeting women may be while exercising. In retrospect, this conclusion may be more valid for fit, athletic engineers[32] than for those whose physiques betray their appreciation of fermented beverages.

Hopefully, you get the idea by now. Make the power of N work for you by asking out more women, and you can increase your chances. Remember Ken Griffey and his puny average. Remember that.

---

[32] It's a theoretical possibility ...

A few comments on Rejection anxiety.

One of the biggest reasons why engineers are unsuccessful at dating is because of overanalysis and rejection anxiety. Generally, engineers are highly analytical people, and the tendency is to go into more scenario and risk assessment analysis before talking to a woman in a bar than George Bush did before he invaded Iraq. Well, maybe that's not a good example. A better way to say this: if you can learn to approach talking to a woman with the same carefree abandon with which George Bush starts major wars, you will both simplify your life and improve your chances. Sure, you'll get rejected, humiliated, embarrassed, ridiculed and probably kicked out of many establishments. But the alternative is to accept failure without trying, just to preserve your dignity. Take a leaf out of George Bush's book: don't worry that 99% of the people you know think you're an idiot. If you wanted to preserve your dignity, you shouldn't have become an engineer in the first place, should you?

A footnote on Statistics

We are of course playing fairly fast and dirty with statistics, mainly because neither of were stats majors, so we probably know just enough to be misleading, but isn't this why statistics were invented in the first place? So if you are a statistician who is really pissed off because we are not following the rules, then we deeply apologise and will issue you a complimentary copy of "Dating for Statisticians" due for release in early 2012 (+/- 2 yrs.). It's highly likely (98.4% probability) that you'll still be single and in need of this book then.

The Sweet Smell of Success

One of the most successful means of attracting women is to be dating a woman. This is just one of a series of cliches such as the chicken and egg, success breeds success, the rich get richer and so on. We may deal with this topic in the chapter titled "Multiple Dating Situations." For now, remember that *appearing to* be dating other women can also help you to get more dates. A woman whose first reaction would be to vomit violently in your direction if you approached her and asked her out might, on believing that you were dating another woman and hence had some minimal credibility, simply refuse to go out with you with a standard rejection line (e.g. "I can't go out with you because my psychic recently put me in touch with my great-great-grandmother and she says that I should only date men from Iowa") with only minimal indications of nausea.

Figure 7.1 A photographer's interpretation of the Beauty of N.
(somewhat gratuitous, but who cares?)

Chapter 8   Increasing Your Native Attractiveness

Though the previous assessment of engineers as potential cohorts might be somewhat discouraging, the good news is that you are not like everyone else, you are unique (well probably, anyway). As an individual, you have a potential to dramatically change your attractiveness level in a way that would not be possible for engineers as a general class of citizenry. The role of self-determination will play a critical role in this chapter, as we aim to bring you above the level of your not-so-attractive compatriots.

The best analogy is to consider yourself as any other product in the market, whether it be a bar of soap, a roll of paper towels or laundry detergent. Of course, you are going to likely be the off-brand equivalent, the ACME brand whereas your non-engineering colleagues will be Tide® or Bounty® or Dial®. It is simply the lot of the engineer not to have the same great hair or smooth talking that goes with the name brands.

So what is the difference between products that are considered "good" and products that are considered "bad"? Some of this has to do simply with marketing, of course and outrageous spending on advertising. Unfortunately, Tiger Woods isn't likely to be sporting a t-shirt with your picture emblazoned on it anytime soon. That leaves us with the other way to improve the perception and attractiveness of a product, which is to make it better. No matter what the initial deficit, improved product quality can help to swing the decision. Consider how many butts are wiped with generic toilet paper instead of Charmin, and you get the idea the little guy can win.

"Better" is just a non-engineering euphemism for increasing the key quality factors and reducing their variability. In laundry detergent, for example, the key quality factors are:

- Removing stains
- Dissolving properly
- Sudsing
- Etc.

Just as careful chemical engineering and formulation can make a detergent better, so can some simple attention to personal behaviour and appearance make YOU better.

The question is, what are the key quality factors that make up your attractiveness. Here are some to start with:

- Appearance, physical
- Appearance, clothing
- Income potential
- Odor, or preferably lack thereof

Just as it takes two to tango, it take two to complete a purchasing transaction. Analysis of the purchasing transaction can also be boiled down to some quite simple concepts:

- Target value
- Lower Specification Limit
- Upper Specification Limit (seldom used in this case)
- Acceptance probability

Most of you will probably recognize the Gaussian distribution despite the bad diagram below; what may be unfamiliar is its application to acceptance criteria in a dating situation. The distribution represents the distribution of minimum target acceptance level of all the women (excluding minors, nuns and retirees, unless you are into that sort of thing).

Figure 8.1   A Somewhat Gaussian distribution

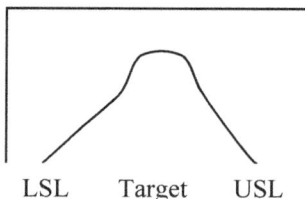

LSL   Target   USL

The basic idea is that a woman, upon meeting a man with the Targeted specification, will be willing to sleep with him. As that key characteristic deviates from the Target, the probability of acceptance (i.e. sex) drops off in a Gaussian fashion. That is to say, at a deviation of 1 sigma, the probability of acceptance drops to 62%. If you are 3 sigma off target, 99.74% of women will reject you.[33]

This picture is clearly over simplified, as there will generally be multiple target specifications. For example, appearance, intelligence, odour, will all contribute to an overall attractiveness factor. That is, just because a guy is good looking does not immediately mean that he will get to have sex with any woman... just most.

Just as there is a distribution in the acceptability criteria, there is also a distribution in performance. Try as they may at Lever to make every bottle of Whisk[34] identical, there will always be small deviations in parameters such as viscosity, pH, sudsing, and so on. It is simply the nature of processes to have variance, whether it be from inadequate temperature control, changes in raw materials, or operators that have had a few too many beers before going on night shift. These things all conspire to introduce variability, and make one bottle of Whisk different from the next. Though we shouldn't let this secret out to the public, lest they start to demand refunds.

From a human standpoint, the performance variability is manifested in several ways. For instance, there are days when you wake up, look in the mirror and say, "wow, I look great today". Okay, so that happened only once in the 1990's, however it emphasises the fact that each of us and each of our characteristics have variability.

The real question is how the mapping of performance characteristics (you) match up with the acceptability criteria (potential partner). The situation with most engineers is the following:

---

[33] Careful readers will note here that we've treated the situation as symmetrical, whereas in reality obviously the situation of being below acceptable is very very different from being above acceptable. To resolve this dilemma, either imagine these as 1-sided Gaussian distributions or, if you're less mathematically adept, try to imagine a world in which women frequently said to each other "that guy is too attractive, no way I'd sleep with him". See further discussion of this point below in the text.

[34] Assuming that is that Lever actually make Whisk, which we can't be bothered to check. It's pretty safe to assume that if they don't, then they don't lose too much sleep trying to ensure that every bottle of it is identical.

Figure 8.2 Acceptance Criteria

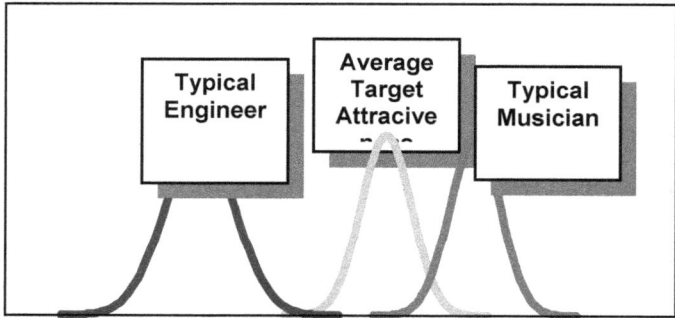

As the chart shows, the performance characteristics of the engineer overlap in only a small region with the acceptability profile of the potential partner. In some cases, the area of overlap is vanishingly small. For example, if your average performance level is 3 standard deviations (3 Sigma) away from the target value, then your chances of getting laid are approximately the same as your chances of being hit by a meteorite.

(Some may argue that Beysian statistics are more relevant for this case since data are not necessarily continuous, e.g. you either get to first base or you don't. However, if a large enough space is sampled, then we can treat the data as continuous.)   Also, it might be argued that the USL is meaningless, for example, that the distribution should be one sided. The engineering argument is "no one is too rich or too thin." However, there is evidence to the existence of a USL, see for example the film "Trop Belle pour Toi" and the fact that many beautiful women are seldom asked out, or at least so they say, though their calendars do tend to fill up rapidly if the alternative is a date with an engineer.

Though quantitative assessment of the target specification and your average performance levels are not as explicit as might be determinable as, for example, a manufacturing process, anecdotal evidence should tell you where your current performance levels are. For example, if you are getting laid by beautiful women on a regular basis, then your average performance level is likely well above the LSL of the acceptance criteria for your audience. The fact that you have purchased this book indicates that this might not be the case. So the question is, what can we do about it.

Raising your average performance

There a lot of ways in which you can raise your average performance levels in measurable ways. These fall into two categories, sustainable and artificially enhanced. Just as drugs and blood doping have long been used by professional athletes for performance enhancement, so too can other artificial, chemical means be used to enhance attractiveness.

For example:

- Hygiene: Take regular showers, brush your teeth... with toothpaste, clip your nails
- Clothes: Wear colours that resemble each other, pay attention especially to footwear.
- Appearance: Working out, regular aerobic exercise, haircuts that cost more than $6
- Cologne: We regard the use of cologne to be the equivalent of the use of steroids for enhancement of attractiveness. You generally have to be fairly desperate to resort to their use, and the results are unpredictable and with potentially grave side effects. It has been well documented that the Society of Professional Engineers, the American Institute of Chemical Engineers and the American Society of Mechanical Engineers have all banned the use of cologne by members, citing the "loss of perceived credibility" due to associations of cologne with used car salesmen and advertising executives. However, if you are desperate, maybe it's worth a shot.

If all of these measures are taken together, then your attractiveness level can likely be raised by one standard deviation, that is one sigma. Assuming the case that your original average performance level was off target by 3 sigma, and that now you are now only 2 sigma away, this means that your chances of scoring that hot chick at the coffee shop have improved to the point that you're now about as likely to get laid as you are to get hit by a bus – significantly more probable than being hit by a meteorite[35] !

---

[35] Actually, we did look up the numbers. Assuming a 1-sided distribution, at 3 standard deviations below the target acceptance level, your chances of getting laid are 0.13%, or just above one in a thousand. By moving to 2 standard deviations below target, your chances increase to 2.27%, a relative increase of over 1700%! If we assume a 2-sided distribution (as in, too attractive is just as bad as not attractive enough, then we get the numbers 0.26% and 4.5% respectively).

Of course, your actual chances do not change if you choose a two-sided distribution – Lord knows, we've tried that one! The problem is that in changing the definition of the curve, you're going to change the definitions of the mean and the standard deviation and everything else as well. We won't go into the details, but you can be sure that if this type of

This is of course terrific news, but the basic problem is that your absolute probability of scoring is still very small, only about 2.27%[36]. That means your chances with that hot babe are not very good.

Of course this analysis says nothing about your own acceptability criteria. It has been known to be the case that a (male) engineer, has refused to sleep with a woman because she did not meet his acceptability criteria. However, since this phenomenon is quite rare, and again, you have purchased (or been given) this book, we will not treat that exceptional circumstance here.

The situation again looks fairly dire, except when you again to look at the beauty of statistics, in particular the beauty of N, and remember how many women there are out there …

---

statistical operation were actually capable of doubling our chances of getting laid, all males would have been born with a genetially ingrained understanding of statistics, which it's pretty safe to say, isn't the case.

[36] However, recall that this 2.27% (or 4.5%) really refers only to the chances that the woman will not reject you based on your attractiveness alone – there is still much work to be done – however, that's a subject for another chapter (or for the sequel).

Chapter 9   Marketing Principles for the Engineer

The bulk of this section has been focused on the dating success probability model, but there is one aspect of dating which eludes both mathematical description and logic, and that is marketing. Non-engineers, especially those in large corporations, tend to view marketers with a great deal of reverence as they are the ones left with making key strategic decisions such as product attributes and sales forecasts. The tendency is to assume that marketers are the only ones who can read the tea leaves or consult the Oracle of Delphi and have access to this arcane information. The purpose of this chapter is to demystify marketing and show how its principles can used for your benefit.

To illustrate the relevance of an understanding of key marketing concepts, let us begin with a wholly inappropriate example. Imagine yourself to be a Jaguar car, with a sale price of $120,000. Now, how many of the people you know would be willing to pay that much for a car which holds only two people, can't be driven on bumpy, pot-holed roads, and is almost guaranteed to triple the number of speeding tickets you get? Probably nobody. Yet the Jaguar company thrives, (as long as you don't consider the fact that they are owned by Ford Motor Company, which booked a $11B loss in 2006). By looking at how they succeed, you can learn some lessons which, despite the obvious differences between Jaguar's place in the world of cars and your place in the world of humans, will still be of practical use.

There are three fundamental lessons, which we will consider one by one.

Identifying a small but non-zero target market.

The makers know that most people could never afford a Jaguar even if they wanted one. But they also know that they don't need to sell a Jaguar to most people to make a profit. The population of the world is over 6 billion. At the price at which they sell their cars, it's likely that they could make a profit by just selling, for example, 600 cars/year. To achieve this, they would need to sell one Jaguar every year to one person out of every ten million. Even if we limit ourselves to consumers in the developed world with drivers licences, they could succeed by selling one Jaguar to every one-millionth person every year.

Viewed in this light, the challenge of selling Jaguars seems a lot less difficult. But neither is it trivial. Because to make it work, they have to find ways to identify and target these consumers. It's not efficient to advertise on TV if there are only 5 or 10 people in the country who might ever even consider buying your product. Nor is it appropriate to just sit around and hope that these few people will chance upon a Jaguar showroom just as they're asking themselves what type of car they should buy next.

Without getting into the specific techniques Jaguar may use, be it targeted direct marketing, product placements or whatever, let us immediately consider the analogous situation of the single engineer. He (or she), in looking for a partner, is faced with a world in which, just like someone selling a Jaguar, there do not appear to be any interested buyers out there. Yet, the engineer has even better odds that Jaguar. Because he doesn't need to find 600 partners, or to convince them to part with $120,000 each. He just needs to find one, out of the 3 billion available of the gender of his/her choice – let's say 1 billion when we exclude underaged and already married people[37]. The rules of probability mean that having such a large number of prospective partners changes the game dramatically in the engineer's favour, if he/she approaches the problem correctly. To put this in perspective, if you buy one billion lottery tickets, you would expect to win the jackpot several times.[38] In the game of relationships, you only need to hit the jackpot once.[39]

---

[37] and we do!!

[38] Note to non-engineers: Just in case you are thinking of taking this suggestion literally, be sure not to buy them all for a single drawing, as you will just end up splitting the jackpot with yourself many times over …
Note to Business Graduates; Also, don't buy them all with the same numbers.

[39] In later chapters we will explain how you might want to hit it more than once, and how you might manage this, but for this chapter we'll keep this assumption for simplicity.

Now, again, let's consider the situation of someone selling Jaguars. If they want to identify a target audience, they might look at simple questions, like is the person rich, is he/she interested in good cars, does he/she live in an area with good roads, and so on. Based on this, instead of wasting money on television advertising, Jaguar could, for example, choose to place some print advertising in up-market car-magazines sold in southeast England.

Now, the engineer, faced with an analogous challenge, needs to find an analogous solution. The male engineer, for example, may hang out mostly with other engineers, who are mostly male, and go to bars only to watch football, where again the clientele will be mostly male. If his objective is to meet a female, this is an example of targeting a sample which is too small to allow a significant probability of success. Or he may frequent up-market bars where there are lots of attractive women who like well-dressed, suave, charming men. This is an example of not selecting an appropriate (realistic) target.

So, what might be a more appropriate target? Actually, this question is not as trivial as it might appear. A defeatist (or a realist) might decide to focus immediately on desperate or unattractive partners, to increase the probability of success. A valid strategy, but as we are only in Chapter 9, we would expect you to be filled with a (unjustified) optimism that you can do better than that, and actually find a partner that you will find at least somewhat attractive. Similarly, while the option of going to an agency to find a Russian or Mongolian or whatever bride may sound interesting – and of course, don't let us stop you – we hope that even if you do this, you will be looking to find someone with whom there is a mutual attraction rather than just desperation on one side (or both).

Our immediate idea was to search the internet to identify groups of "attractive men and women who want to date engineers", but a very thorough search yielded no helpful results, although there were some interesting options for engineers who were highly aggressive and violent midgets, or who weigh over 690 lbs, or who have extremely large hands and feet, among other ideas. We will encourage those few engineers in a position to take advantage of these possibilities to do so, but we recognize that for the rest of you, no such easy answer may be available. There simply are not a whole lot of people out there who, without further encouragement, want to date engineers.

But fear not, because again thinking of the Jaguar example, how many people who had never seen or read about a Jaguar would spontaneously pay $120,000 for one? Not many. This is where the second and third steps of our Market Research Techniques come into play.

Understanding Your Target Consumers

It is fair to say that not many single women go home each evening wishing that instead of their empty apartment they would find an engineer waiting for them. Unfortunately, the human brain is simply not capable of this type of logical fallacy. However, perhaps unconsciously, the woman may desire some of the traits that an engineer might possess. For example, she might wish there were somebody in her house who would be able to calculate the likely worth of her house in 20 years assuming the housing market would increase at a compound rate of 2% per annum while the condition of her house would decay at about 1% per annum, but that she would spend 13% of the value of the house on major reconstruction work after 15 years. Or she may have a leaking pipe and wish there were someone who could explain to her that this was probably due to the pressure inside the pipe being higher than the pressure outside the pipe, so that the water leaks out rather than air leaking in, and that if she wanted to eliminate the leak, she should call a plumber.

The engineer needs to grasp at every straw like this. But rather than grasp at the straws individually, he needs to wait until they have achieved a critical mass, and then present himself as the solution to all her worldly worries. Of course the probability of success will be low, but remember that you only have to succeed one time in a billion.

Again, turning to the Jaguar example, but imagining ourselves to be starting from scratch, how would the Jaguar manufacturer proceed? Assuming they didn't believe themselves omniscient, the first thing they would do would be to try to understand why some prospective consumers might (or might not) buy a Jaguar. To give an oversimplified example, they might begin with the assumption that some people would pay $120,000 for a super driving experience. But the potential consumers would tell them that no matter how good the car might be, the level of traffic, the speed limits and the quality of the roads severely limited how good the driving experience for them could ever be, and it would never be worth paying $120,000 for. However, the same people might tell them that they might be willing to pay that much for a car that would be a real status symbol. And they might say that they would buy a Jaguar rather than, say, a Ferrari, if they believed that that would give them the image of being patriotic Britons, proud of British engineering[40], or whatever.

And so, Jaguar would know that, while they still had to deliver a great driving experience, the secret of selling the cars in South East England might be less about the car *per se*, and more about the image that the car

---

[40] Sorry, that kind of sarcasm is not appropriate in a book which some British engineers might actually buy. (Ed.)

possessed. And so instead of spending $1000 per car on an ultra-sophisticated windshield wiper, they might spend this money on a product placement in a James Bond movie, where he would drive off into the sunset with a beautiful Kenyan spy in a Jaguar, chased by pursuers in foreign cars, and as he pulled away from them, he might comment that you just couldn't beat British cars. The point being, that at some point, somebody had to actually understand that this was what potential Jaguar consumers wanted, and this could be a selling point.

The obvious difficulty with applying this logic to engineers is that engineers are certainly not the Jaguars of the dating world. However, surprisingly, for once their analytical skills, so useless in so many other aspects of social life, can be helpful here. While it might be difficult for an engineer to meet enough single women, or to understand them when he does, the engineer can easily begin by talking with those women he does know, single or otherwise. They will give him helpful hints about things like changing socks occasionally, centre-partings, brown shoes and other things that women find important. And they might also give him some clues about qualities he possesses, despite being an engineer, which some women might find positive. For example "you still have a lot of your hair", "your apartment is in a nice location", "you make three times as much money as most guys I know", "you were able to explain global warming to my idiot friend who voted for Bush" or whatever ...

Having collected this knowledge, we come to the third element of using Market Research Techniques to improve your dating life:

Optimise and Sell your Benefit

In the case of Jaguar, having decided that they wanted their cars to be positioned as British status symbols, this then becomes the "benefit", in marketing parlance, of the Jaguar. In the example above the James Bond placement would be one way they might sell this benefit – another might be to let the price of their cars be widely known so that their status symbol value would be increased – or even, instead of having a selling price of, say, £80,000, they could make their official selling price 110,000, but give £30,000 pounds in "rebates" or "incentives" – which would still leave the public, whom the buyer wants to impress, thinking he has paid £110,000 for the car.[41]

---

[41] This isn't as irrational as it seems, and it's actually rooted deeply into our brains through evolution. Rather than thinking (logically) "what idiot would spend that much for a car?", a potential mating partner is more likely to think "he must be really rich if he can afford to waste that much on a car". Engineers have a lot to learn about this way of thinking – something that male peacocks have always understood. Peacock engineers typically have

In the case of the engineer, taking as an example the comments above, he might decide to build on the positives of his apartment, his salary and his understanding of environmental chemistry. For example, by getting involved with a group of people working to protect the environment against soon to be ex-president Bush and ex-vice-president Cheney who are happy to mortgage our future to keep their industry buddies happy today, the engineer might invite a group of them, ideally involving some single women, of course, to hold their monthly meetings at his apartment[42], and impress them by providing them with top-quality food and drink, all of course being biologically, ecologically sound and whatever else might be important to the group. The key here is that while he is still an engineer with all the attendant flaws that that entails, some of the women in the group may in fact see primarily his positive traits, and may be sufficiently blinded by these to initially overlook the flaws.

Again, we're not talking very good odds here, but by applying these techniques, you can more effectively both find your target audience and find the most promising way to target them.

However, realistically, this probably won't work without a lot more help, which is why we'd recommend that you read the rest of the book before applying any of this directly – we don't want to be held responsible for Market Research agencies around the country being bombed by Women's Rights groups.

---

small, unimpressive tail feathers, because large tails are inefficient. Peacock Humanities majors have large impressive tail feathers and get much more sex than the peacock engineers – this is part of the reason why, as evolution has progressed, peacocks have gotten increasingly dim.

[42] Which he would clean beforehand, and ideally have a female acquaintance check it was really clean.

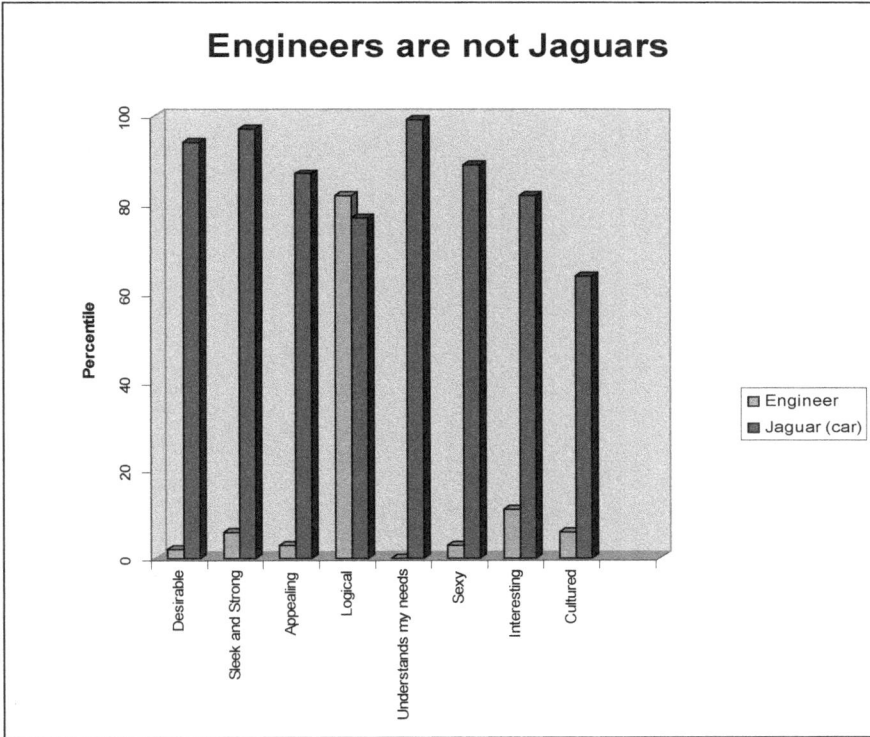

Figure 9.1 The authors' great optimism about some of the ideas presented in this chapter was somewhat tempered by the results of a study among a sample of 142 women, who were asked, in separate questionnaires, to rate different types of cars on a set of 8 criteria, and then to rate men in different careers on the same criteria. It is seen that while Jaguars are seen to score very highly, Engineers do somewhat less well. This data has led some to question the theoretical (and moral) validity of making any analogy between Engineers and Jaguars. The authors cannot comment on this due to a pending legal action by the Jaguar Brand and the Ford Motor Company (who are obviously pretty desperate for any cash they can get their hands on…).

Section D: The Mechanics of Dating

A Step by Step Approach

Chapter 10: How To Ask for a Date

As engineers we are often prone to overanalysis. When an engineer typically thinks about dating, he develops anxious tics in his face, his throat tightens and acne breaks out on all visible surfaces. What is usually happening is the mental development of a huge fault tree of various terrible things that could happen as a result of asking a woman out on a date. These fears range from being beaten up by a current boyfriend to being ridiculed in the local newpaper, events which actually happen far less than 50% of the time.

So to follow our thorough presentation of an analytical approach to dating in the previous section, we now come to deal with the actual hands-on (hopefully) mechanics of dating. We hope to present a highly detailed, step-by-step approach that you can follow for practically any situation that you might encounter in dating, up to and including sex.

It begins, of course, with asking a woman out on a date. Ultimately, the engineer must realize that asking a woman on a date is much less complex than solving a dynamics problem or writing a subroutine in Fortran. To illustrate the point, the following flowchart has been painstakingly developed by the authors to describe a dating algorithm. We recommend that the reader make a copy, have it laminated, and use it as a guide for future dating actions.

We begin at the top, with target identification, the details of which are in the next chapter. It should be noted, however, that even random target identification can potentially yield good results. The second step is to approach the target, preferably without a large caliber sidearm, (although this depends on the cultural environment), and in as non-threatening a way as possible. If the target flees at high velocity, that is, faster than you can jog comfortably, then it is preferable to break pursuit and seek a new target.

Next comes perhaps the most difficult psychological barrier to overcome, which is saying "hello" to the target. In future versions of this book, we will develop a multimedia training module on this element to capture all of the key verbal and nonverbal elements of the "hello". For now, we assume that you are able to get through this step. The response in this step is also critical, as it can range from acceptance, to flight, to threatening behavior. So it is important that you pay attention to whether or not the woman in question is reaching into her purse for a condom or for a large can of mace.

The rest of the flowsheet is quite systematic, and we leave the exercise of writing the "small talk" subroutine to the reader. One hint would be to record portions of daytime television programming for clues on how to best execute small talk. For clues on how to best put together a begging subroutine, spend some time with a friend who has small children.

Figure 10.1 Date
Asking Flowchart

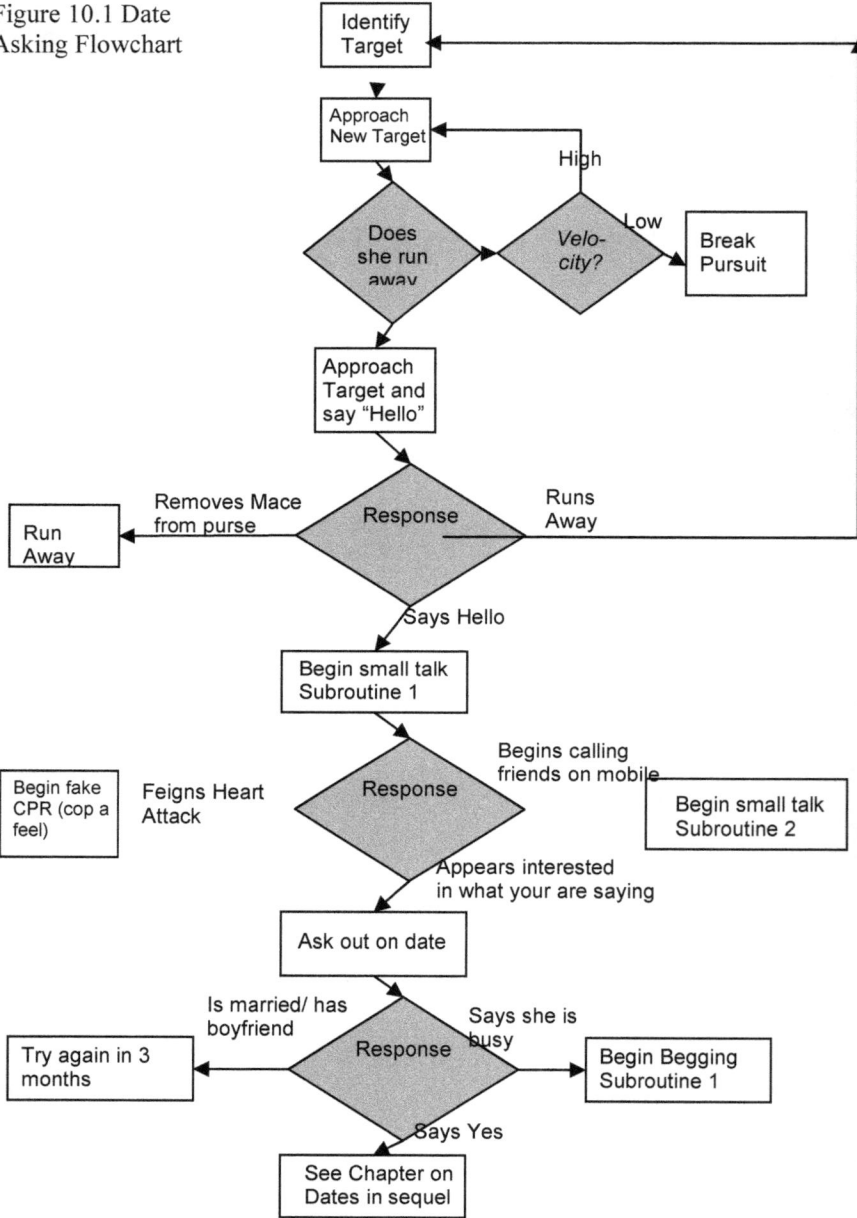

Chapter 11   The Eigenvector Model of Evaluating prospective Dates

---

Now that you know *How* to ask a woman on a date, the natural question is *Who* to ask[43]. In previous chapters we've demonstrated convincingly that your situation isn't logically as hopeless as it might seem. Yet, reality tells you that it still feels pretty hopeless. And as you begin to venture into conversations with women, let's again be realistic and admit that you're likely to get some pretty embarrassing rejections.

One consolation for all of us is that there's only so far down your image and self-confidence can fall before they hit rock bottom, and you're probably pretty close already. In this context, the secret lies not so much in minimising the embarrassment as in failing gloriously.

In other words, if you're going to get blown off in front of all your friends, work colleagues or favourite pocket protector, at least get blown off by a woman you find attractive. Which brings us to the subject of this chapter – how to calculate how attractive a woman is to you.

We all know the problem. You walk into a bar, you see a woman sitting alone. You know that as soon as she sees you, she'll probably run screaming out the door. But there is the moment where she hasn't noticed you yet, where, if you can find a way to start a conversation with her, she just might be too polite to scream as she's running, and that would certainly be a boost for your morale.

The problem is, you can't decide if she's really your type. She's maybe blonde and voluptuous and sexy, but you just can't remember if that's the kind of woman you prefer.

And then, while you're still pondering this, she spots you and the usual screaming exit follows.

In this chapter we'll teach you how to avoid this source of embarrassment (but not several others) by always having a quick and easy numerical technique to decide whether a woman is attractive or not – and

---

[43] And if your reaction to this question is "that should be '*whom* to ask'", then this will be really tough for you ..

indeed, if used with sufficient precision, to rank them in order so that you can quickly decide which of two women is more attractive – although this latter technique is of limited value for most engineers, being applicable usually only in situations where social conventions or physical impediments prevent women from escaping from their attentions. Examples where this can be useful include formal dinners at Buckingham Palace and visitors' hour on the high-security row of Deerborn women's prison in Texas.[44]

I think it's fair to say that immediately a question regarding the attractiveness of a lady arises, any engineer will immediately think in terms of linear algebra, n-dimensional vector spaces and matrix analysis. Clearly the challenge is to paramaterise the lady, and how better to do this than with a set of n mutually-independent vectors delineating an n-dimensional vector space. It is optional whether you choose to make these vectors orthogonal[45] or not, the final result should not change, however, it may give more clarity, which would perhaps justify the additional work needed – more practically, it may be a further reason to postpone the actual interface with a real woman ...

However, for some of the agricultural engineers reading this, the application to women might not be as evident as the ovine application, so to avoid any confusion, let's briefly describe the technique.

Phase 1: Definition of your personal preferences matrix

In layman's terms, there are several steps involved in this, which can be summarised as:

- Identify the key parameters which may be important to you in quantifying the appeal of a woman. You don't actually have to be sure if they are important to you our not, the analysis will tell you this. Be sure to include a range of both positive and negative characteristics. Let the number of parameters be n. These can be

---

[44] Some readers of a previous edition of this book who ventured to try out this technique complained of confusion between these two locations. The engineer who asked her magesty what she was in for escaped with only a minor rebuke, but the one who agreed to be knighted by one of the ladies on death-row is now missing one of his ears. [Surely the authors could have thought of a slightly less predictable joke, you might think, but that would be forgetting that they are engineers .. (Ed.)]

[45] Examples of relatively orthogonal vectors might be height and IQ, for example. Examples of non-orthogonal vectors might be eye-colour and hair-colour, where clearly on average those with darker hair are more likely to have brown eyes, and those with lighter hair more likely to have blue eyes. But our mathematical techniques will work also for these non-orthogonal vectors. Difficulties may arise with vectors that are very closely correlated, such as height and shoe-size, which may be an issue for those who find shoe-size of great importance in choosing a potential date.

such things as hair colour, intelligence or ability to program machine code with her left hand while fixing a puncture with her right.

- Identify at least *n* examples of women. In the first edition, we lost a lot of readers at this point, so let me emphasise, you do not have to know these women. In fact, to protect us in case of legal challenge, let it be said that we in no way encourage you to try to get to know women at this early stage of your training. (Forget everything you read in the Statistics chapter about the power of *N*). However it has been seen to be more practical if you focus on real living women rather than characters in computer games.

- Try to give each of the n women you've identified a numerical attractiveness score, which should be somewhere in the range 0-100. As this is intended as a linear process, your scores should approximate a Gaussian distribution, corresponding to the true variation among real women. To give an example, you might give Beyonce' a score of 90 and your boss a score of 9, but try to get about 2/3 of the women in the range of 30-70.

- Then, for each of the women, attribute a score for each of the *n* parameters you've identified. This sounds like a lot of work, especially if *n* is a large number, but remember, it's not as if you have a life anyhow, so this is probably going to be time spent relatively productively compared to the alternatives open to you.

This should give you a set of linear equations in the form $Ax = y$, where A_{ij} are the coordinates of the *nxn* matrix corresponding to the scores of each woman on the *n* quantities you've identified, while the y_i are the total scores of each woman. Solving this equation by simple matrix operations allows you to identify the column vector *x* which will then allow you to calculate the attractiveness of any woman by simply evaluating her on all the key factors that you have identified and multiplying by *x*, by simple vector multiplication.

This process can be repeated to get an increasingly accurate model anytime another woman is encountered, either by adding in more factors (so generating an *n+1 x n+1* matrix) or by eliminating one of the women, for whom the data available or the overall assessment is felt to be less accurate. Alternatively, new women can be used to validate the existing model.

Example:
We'll work with $n = 3$ to simplify, in reality *n* needs to be larger. Consider the case where an engineer decides that the three most important qualities a lady needs to possess for her to be an ideal date are:

- having the most advanced software on her palm pilot
- not being too tall
- liking to talk about the intricacies of Gödel's Theorem for hours.

Let's assume that the engineer knows three women, whom he calls P, Q and R (since they won't tell him their real names). For each of the three he defines their scores on the three criteria as follows:

$a1$ = number of weeks since palm-pilot software was issued
$a2$ = 230 − (height in cm)
$a3$ = minutes can listen to him talk about theorem without interrupting, yawing, snoring.

With these analyses, he calculates the scores for each of the three women as follows:

	a1	*a2*	*a3*
P	*50*	*80*	*10*
Q	*10*	*60*	*60*
R	*30*	*60*	*80*

And he also estimates the overall attractiveness of the three as follows:

$$P = 35$$
$$Q = 80$$
$$R = 70$$

With this information, it's not possible to solve for *x*, the desired vector, as follows:

$$\begin{vmatrix} 50 & 80 & 10 \\ 10 & 60 & 60 \\ 30 & 60 & 80 \end{vmatrix} \times \begin{vmatrix} x1 \\ x2 \\ x3 \end{vmatrix} = \begin{vmatrix} 35 \\ 80 \\ 70 \end{vmatrix}$$

Leading to the solution:

$$x = \begin{vmatrix} -1 \\ 1 \\ 0.5 \end{vmatrix}$$

Phase 2: Evaluation of new women

Now, using this matrix, the attractive of any female can be evaluated, using just the three simple data points: For example, let's say he meets a woman, S, whose palm pilot is 30 weeks old, who is 5'3 tall (= 160 cm) and who can listen to him talk about Godel's theorem for 40 minutes before yawning. He can do a quick matrix multiplication to calculate that her attractiveness is 60, therefore, she is above-averagely attractive, although not spectacular. Based on this number, he can decide immediately whether to approach her or not, knowing that his decision is based on a solid mathematical rationale. For example, if the alternative women in the bar all score below 40, and if the only alternative to talking to one of them is to hang out with one of his colleagues (who, while scoring highly on the above criteria, loses 200 points for being male), he would probably choose to approach her.

Once you have completed this analysis for yourself and validated the approach, you will be amazed at how effectively it facilitates decisions about whom to approach, which of various prospective dates to choose, and so forth. (In Chapter 13 we will discuss the mathematics of dating more than one person, but that in no way invalidates this analysis, as the need to prioritise will still arise).

Figure 11.1 Test your attractiveness evaluation algorithm. Looking at the photographs of the six attractive ladies above, fill in the input parameters to your model, based on the extent of your knowledge, and put in estimated values for parameters for which you do not have data. Then calculate the relative attractiveness of the six ladies above, fill in their values beside their pictures above, and see if your model correctly predicts your order of preference.

<u>Worked Example</u>[46]

Use this page to work through an example of an Eigenvector model, using data from real women.

---

[46] In reality this page accidentally was left blank during the editing, and we couldn't be bothered renumbering all the pages in the Contents ..

Chapter 12   Competitive Dating Situations, or How the Cuban Missile Crisis can Help You Score Dates

You're slowly adapting to the difficulties of simply communicating with a woman. You've even learned how to figure out whether you find her attractive or not. Then comes the shock that even if you are psychologically and intellectually adjusted enough to manage this, there's no guarantee that she'll be willing to communicate with you. And now, even before you're had the time to adjust to that shock, comes yet another. The most challenging aspect of dating may not be either of the above, but rather it may derive from the fact that dating is a competitive activity. In other words, women are what is technically known as "scarce", and men must compete even for the "privilege" of trying to convince them that they should just consider the bare possibility of communicating with you – and we're still a long way short of sex here (in case that's not obvious).

For the purposes of this chapter, let us assume that you've completed the preliminaries of the previous chapters, and so have maximised your attractiveness (to the extent that has been possible, which, let's be realistic, probably wasn't much) and you've analysed the attractiveness of a particular woman and concluded that you find her attractive, using the matrix analysis method and your personal validated matrix.

To simplify, without loss of generality, we will also assume that we're dealing with a real, living woman, and not one with whom your only interaction is paying by credit card to access her website. For example, let's say it's a woman who works in another department of your company or studies in another department in your college, whom you see only in the canteen at lunch time, and to whom you have never talked. (we don't want to make the challenge too difficult by dealing with how to undo all the damage you've surely done if you have talked to her before reading this book).

Furthermore, without loss of generality, let's call this woman Esmeralda, although once you find out her real name, you might want to use that instead – what a pity if you were to ruin everything by yelling out "Esmeralda!" at a critical moment of love-making, and realistically there's no way she'd believe your explanation, and if you actually show her this book, she may believe she's been exploited, and the damage could be even worse ...

Now, having calculated that you find Esmeralda attractive, this chapter will deal with the steps you need to take to ensure that Esmeralda decides that she would prefer to date you than to date any of her other suitors.

Some of you will recall that we briefly touched on this problem in Chapter 0, but did not outline the specific steps to the solution.

Let us without loss of generality make the assumption that there are n other suitors, and that each of them is physically more attractive than you, dresses better than you, and is personally more charming than you. Let us further assume that it is not realistic for you to address any of these factors within the timeframe of the process. Finally, for the purposes of this example, we will assume for simplicity that you are the only engineer and the only person to have studied and applied the techniques outlined in this book.

As stated in Chapter 0, the objective is to convince Esmeralda to date *you*, rather than any of the other n suitors, despite the obvious handicaps. To simplify the example, let us define your objective precisely as being that Esmeralda should accompany you to a high profile date, e.g. formal dance or hot ticket concert, in 3 weeks time, while the other n candidates would each like her to accompany them.

When faced with any competitive situation like this, the engineer should first seek for a solution in the area of game theory. Very briefly, game theory is the theory of games.

Perhaps that introduction was a little too brief to be helpful, so here's a more long-winded one:

Game theory is a mathematical treatment of any situation where two or more people have objectives which may be at odds. There are many example of game theory with which the reader is probably familiar.

- A classic example in which game theory was used is the Cuban missile crisis, when President Kennedy wanted to stop the Soviet Union putting missiles on Cuba. He did not want to start a nuclear war, but at the same time, he knew that only the threat of a war would actually stop the Soviets putting the missiles there. It was a very high-stakes "game", in which he had to find a "strategy" which would use the threat of a war to prevent the missile deployment, but would not actually lead to a war.

- Another classic example of game theory is the "prisoners' dilemma" game, in which two people who have just committed a crime are captured and interviewed separately by the police. If they both stay silent, they can both escape with 1-year sentences – but if one of them chooses to implicate the other, while the other stays silent, then he will get off scot free and the other will go to jail for 5 years. If they both implicate each other, they both go to jail for 3 years.

We will not get into the analyses of these games here, many books have been written about Prisoners Dilemma alone, from angles such as whether it can explain the evolution of cooperative behaviour among humans to angles like where it is theoretically possible to devise an "optimum" strategy.

However, let us use the example of prisoners dilemma above to define the concept of a payoff matrix. To keep the numbers positive, let us consider the "reward" for each player to the the number of years out of the next 5 that he is NOT in jail. If the first number in the brackets represents the payoff for prisoner A and the second that for prisoner B, the payoff matrix looks like:

Strategies	*B stays silent*	*B implicates A*
A stays silent	*(4,4)*	*(0,5)*
A implicates B	*(5,0)*	*(2,2)*

What makes the game so interesting psychologically is that, if this is a once-off game and they will never see each other again, the best strategy (highest payoff) for each player is to implicate the other – and this is true regardless of what the other does. However, if they both do this, they will end up a lot worse off than if they both stay silent. If they could agree on a strategy, they would definitely agree to both stay silent, but playing as "selfish" individuals, is there a way for them to arrive that this strategy?

It is important, though, to highlight one common misconception about game theory, namely that it is somehow amoral. It is true that in the context of each game, it is assumed that each players acts "selfishly" to maximise his own payout. However, it is also true that each player defines his own valuation of the possible outcomes – so there is nothing that says I cannot give value to something other than my own selfish desires. For example, if the two prisoners were brothers, they might each also put high value on not having their brother go to jail. Or they might put value on the honour and respect they would get for staying silent. Game theory assumes that each player has already taken all these factors into account before the payoff matrix has been defined so that it reflects everything that is important to them.

In a simpler example, if the game involved playing soccer with a 5-year-old child, I would probably give a high value to each goal the child scored and no value at all, or even a negative value, to any goals I scored. But having defined that my objective in the game was that the child should win, I would then play "selfishly" to make that happen.[47]

Now, you will ask, why game theory? The answer is simple, and goes back to *Theorem 0.2*, from Chapter 0. While these non-engineers may have all these aesthetic and social advantages, you are smarter than they are. In practical terms, Game Theory will be your tool to turn your superior intelligence and strategic thinking into practical benefits, and so overcome your social deficiencies.

The "games" you will need to play will be of several types, but in the context of this chapter they fall into two categories:

1. games in which the only players are you and one or more of the other suitors.
2. games in which Esmeralda is (also) involved.

Now, with the above caveat that you define your own payout matrix, and so, for example you might find it perfectly appropriate, even desirable, to subject suitor A to public humiliation, but you might, if possible, like to boost suitor B's morale as he is a friend, we're going to assume that you yourself have worked through this and have arrived at a payoff matrix for each game, which we will then assume you will play "selfishly" in order to achieve your ultimate objective of taking Esmeralda on a date. Some of the examples of games we'll give below might not be to your taste, it is entirely up to you to choose your strategy, these are only examples.

Let us first consider the very simplest type of game, which is a zero-sum game. In a zero-sum game, the total payoff is constant, so whatever one player gains, the other(s) lose, keeping the total fixed. In reality these games are very rare. For example, it might seem that for the $n+1$ suitors, the game of convincing Esmeralda is a zero-sum game – the outcome will be that one of them takes her and the other n do not. You must strongly encourage this kind of simplistic thinking in your opponents, but you must never succumb to it yourself !!

For a person looking at this game as a zero-sum game, the pay off schedule might look like this, with the payments normalised so that the total is zero:

---

[47] I saw the game in question, and it looked to me like the 5-year-old won fair and square, despite the author's best efforts – Editor's Note.

Player	Payoff if go with Esmeralda	Payoff if not go with Esmeralda
1	1	-1/n
2	1	-1/n
3	1	-1/n
4	1	-1/n
..	1	-1/n
..	1	-1/n
N	1	-1/n
n+1	1	-1/n

However, this overlooks many factors, and each of these provides opportunities for the engineer to devise a superior strategy.

1. The payoffs will be very different for a player who is already somewhat undecided whether he'd prefer to invite Esmeralda or, for example, his wife – for him, the negative of not going with her will be less negative, and the positive of going with her will be lower. On the other hand, the single guy who has been in love with her for a year and who has absolutely no hope of finding anyone else to invite may have a larger positive and negative scores. And so on. To see how this can help, let us imagine a situation where just these two scores have changed. Obviously it's not a zero-sum game anymore:

Player	Payoff if go with Esmeralda	Payoff if not go with Esmeralda
1	1	-1/n
2	0.1	-0.01
3	100	-100
4	1	-1/n
..	1	-1/n
..	1	-1/n
N	1	-1/n
n+1	1	-1/n

Now, imagine being any player in this game, other than player 3. What is the psychological impact of seeing that player 3 is 100 times more determined to win than you are? In many cases, if used effectively, the effect will be to cause some of the players to withdraw. This can be for good reasons "if he wants her that badly, I suppose I should let him" or cowardly reasons "if I take Esmeralda, what happens the next time I need to get my PC fixed?" (if player 3 works in IT) or whatever. The point is, by letting the other players know that you are significantly more determined to win than they are, even without doing anything else, you can give yourself a significant advantage. There are two key points to remember here, though.

The first is that you do not necessarily need to *be* more determined, you just need to let all your opponents believe that you are. For example, as an engineer, you might let it be known that any other person who takes Esmeralda on the date is going to have his office treated with invisible radioactive material that will give them an 85% chance of developing bowel cancer – they won't know if it's realistic or not. This would not be viewed as immoral behaviour unless you actually do it, until then it's just competing.

The second point, of which more below, is that you *absolutely* must *not* let Esmeralda believe you are determined (she will read this as desperate) to bring her.

2. A second key reason why you should never assume that games are zero-sum is that that typically results from over-simplifying the problem. In this case, even the winner of the game has in reality a range of possibilities – for example a "win" in which Esmeralda agrees to go to the dance with him, but only out of a sense of sympathy, is not quite as good as one where she believes herself to be honoured and fortunate to have won him away from all the other women who would like to bring him. And for the "losers" of this game, it is very different to be seen to have tried and lost with Esmeralda than it is if you still have the possibility, after the "game" to approach somebody else and invite her "as your first choice".

    All of these factors can and should be manipulated. In some cases, it is sufficient to put doubts in a player's head ("you know how she talks! If you ask her and she says no, the rest of the company will know in 10 minutes, and then who will you find?" or "she's a very polite girl – she told me she's not really interested in any of the men here, but she'd feel duty-bound to go if she was asked – I don't think she'd be much fun though.")[48].

---

[48] In all these examples, our objective is to provide the mathematical framework only, we hope that you will be able to come up with more convincing strategies, examples, lines, etc. ...

In other cases, you might want to bribe/threaten/tempt another suitor. ("You know, I heard Esmeralda has an even better-looking sister who's single. I think if I invited Esmeralda, I might be able to set you up with the sister so we could go as a foursome" "You know that if you invite Esmeralda instead of Sally from payroll, Sally says she's going to check every expense report you submit with a fine tooth comb until she finds a reason to reject it").

So, the general lesson on zero-sum games is that, in this kind of context, they probably don't exist. But if your opponents think they're in one, use that to your advantage.

Let now consider one example of a two-person game involving just you and one of the other suitors. It's a very simple game, sometimes called "chicken", which is often described as follows. Two people drive their cars at 80 miles/hour, straight at each other. The person who swerves away first loses. However, if neither player swerves at all, they both die, which is worse than just a loss of honour. The pay off matrix might look something like this:

Strategies	*B goes straight on*	*B swerves*
A goes straight on	*(0,0)*	*(6,3)*
A swerves	*(3,6)*	*(4,4)*

Note how this is totally different from the previous game. In Prisoner's Dilemma, in a once-off game, defecting (informing on your partner) always has the highest payout. Here, however, there is no one strategy that is dominant. If your opponent does not swerve, you would rather lose your honour than your life (at least that's the assumption).

Now, you do not want to put your life and honour on the line in this manner, and even if you did, it's doubtful that anyone would agree to go against you, or that Esmeralda would be remotely impressed. But you can devise more practical versions. For example, let us say that one or the other suitors is Reggie from Accounting. You are working together on a critical project which is due to be delivered the week after the dance, in which your key counterparts are in another time-zone. Without warning Reggie, you can set up a critical project meeting for the Friday of the event, "inadvertently" confusing the times so that instead of being at 4-6 pm in New York, where you live, it is scheduled at 4-6 pm in San Francisco, hence 7-9 pm in New York. And the event starts at 7:30. Now, both you and Reggie know that one of you needs to attend this meeting or the San Francisco company will pull out of the deal, and you will both probably be fired. However, you don't both need to attend.

Figure 12.1 Prisoner's Dilemma. It's unfortunate that this drawing bears almost no relationship to the concept of the Prisoner's Dilemma game, or indeed to anything else in this chapter. However, careful analysis will reveal a connection – the authors, like the players in the game, want to maximise their payoff, and therefore they found it cheaper to just cut and paste and unrelated cartoon – even stretching it out so it would fill the page – rather than pay some poor starving artist a fair price to draw a proper cartoon.

The analogy with the "chicken" game is now clear. Which of you will have the nerve to skip the meeting and ask Esmeralda to the dance, knowing that if the other goes to the dance as well, they will both be fired? And of course, the obvious answer is that you will. Because being much smarter than Reggie, you've already rescheduled the meeting but "forgotten" to put him in copy, and, by using Reggie's total lack of understanding of electronic calendars, you've convinced him that the meeting is going ahead as scheduled and furthermore that both your CEO and the CEO of the San Francisco group will be joining by video conference.[49]

What you've done is to modify the "perceived" payouts for the chicken game. Remember that each player plays the game and chooses his strategy based on how he perceives his payoffs, which may or may not reflect reality. So you've created a truly biased game with a payoff matrix like:

Strategies	*Reggie goes on date with Esmeralda*	*Reggie goes to the meeting*
You go to the dance	*(4,0)*	*(5,4)*
You go to the meeting	*(2,5)*	*(2,3)*

With your knowledge of the true payoffs, you have a "dominant" strategy – no matter what Reggie chooses, you know you are better off going to the dance. This gives you total confidence to out-play Reggie in the game of chicken. Reggie does not have a dominant strategy, his best solution is still to go on the date and have you cover the meeting, but with the mention of the CEO's and with him thinking of the chance to impress them all alone without any engineers around, you've also reduced the relative differences in his payouts. So even if he's not fully convinced that you will not "chicken" out, he's still very tempted to go to the meeting.

Result: at no cost or risk to yourself, you have eliminated one potential suitor.

We neither want to nor believe we could give an exhaustive list of type of games that you could use to eliminate other suitors. By reading any standard text on game theory, you should be able to identify many interesting strategies, and then it's just a case of choosing the right strategy for each person.[50]

---

[49] We repeat the above footnote – this is intended to be demonstrative, not realistic.
[50] And also, of course, remember that you don't have to limit yourself to game theory. When dealing with HR people, for example, it often takes no more than unplugging their LAN connection and telling them the email system is down, so preventing them from

The second type of games you need to consider are games involving Esmeralda. These are by definition much more complex. While with other suitors, your objective is still pretty clear – they should not accompany her on the date – in the case of games involving Esmeralda, a strategy might be unsuitable even if it results in her accompanying you to the event. This could occur, for example, if she feels tricked or if she feels compelled to go with you, against her will. With this in mind, it is difficult to imagine very many simple games (with only a few strategies) which are likely to be relevant. However, that doesn't limit the quality of insights that game theory can give you. To explain, let us imagine a multi-person game, but consider for the moment only the payoffs for you and for Esmeralda. In this example, as Esmeralda is the "scarce" resource, we speak of the suitors inviting her – however, this can equally well work by the suitor creating a situation in which she invites him – the point is, from our view of the game, we are one of the suitors who are choosing strategies with the objective of going on the date with Esmeralda.

Strategies	Esmeralda accepts	Esmeralda declines
You invite Esmeralda	(5,1)	(0,3)
Suitor A asks her	(1,4)	(3,3)
Suitor B asks her	(1,2)	(3,3)
Etc ..		

To read this table, recall that the first number is the payoff for *you*, the second is for Esmeralda. So your payoff is 1 if another player asks her and she accepts (better than you ask her and she declines, but not as good as someone else asks her and she declines, meaning you have one less competitor, maybe).

Now, we've assumed in the above matrix (and it's typically a realistic assumption) that even if she is fundamentally a nice person, she probably doesn't want to go to the dance with you, so ultimately she will be tempted to refuse your invitation, while in the case of some other suitors, she is likely to accept, and others not. [In other words, if Esmeralda had total knowledge of all the suitors who were interested, you would definitely not be the one she would choose. In the absence of this perfect knowledge, she would answer any given invitation based on how it compared with her perceived alternatives.]

---

contacting Esmeralda by email – which might be useful if she suddenly goes out of town. With Marketers, simply unplugging their computer can be equally effective.

Analysing this matrix[51] immediately suggests the two areas on which you must focus.

1. You must find a way to adjust the payoff matrix to the extent that if you ask her, her payoff for accepting will be (or at least appear to her) more positive than that for rejecting you.
2. You must ensure that none of the suitors likely to be accepted get the chance to ask her until you have completed point one and asked her yourself.

There are many ways to approach both of these, and we will give just one example, which kills two birds with one stone. Let us assume that the above matrix is valid 3 weeks before the dance. Now, let's say that in the third last week before the event, most of the inviting takes place. So if we can create a situation in which with only two weeks to go, Esmeralda still has not received any acceptable invitations, this is likely to increase her payoff for accepting and lower her payoff for declining. One way to achieve this can be to eliminate competitors as shown in the chicken game above. Other, more practical ways, can be to create situations where their email doesn't work, to let it be known that she's already accepted to go with you (or someone else, or her linebacker fiance' who is moving to town that week ..). The point is, make sure that in that week, no acceptable candidate invites her to the dance.

The second strategy which, for reasons unknown to men, frequently works with women, is to make yourself appear indifferent to her and much in demand by others. (see the chapter on the Bohr dating model for more on this topic). This does not mean that you do not compliment her or even that you do not flatter her – it just means that you appear to do this because you are nice and because it is true, but not because you have any remote interest in going out with her, since there are all these other interested women who are even more attractive than she is.

Most of us would have great difficulty creating a world where this were true even in our own imaginations, not to mind in somebody else's imagination. But again, careful consideration reveals it to be less challenging than it might at first appear, especially when you recall that this only has to be kept up for a week, and that this is not somebody you see very often.

The first, and probably most difficult, step in all this, is to make her realise that you're ignoring her. Because normally she will pay so little attention to you that it will just seem like a welcome blessing if she doesn't see you for a week. This is a very delicate balance to strike, and realistically 9 times out of 10 you're going to screw it up. But to give you

---

[51] Though recall that you won't have this information nicely tabulated for you in real life.

an example, if you were to meet at the coffee machine one day (obviously it appears coincidental to her), you might strike up a brief conversation about the dance, talk about how the woman you invited last year has left the company[52], and what a great dancer she was. Don't lay it on too thick. Maybe you add a comment like "I suppose you're going with one of the men in Finance." or whatever, but somehow (it's not easy) making it sound like you're totally indifferent – certainly, it must not appear like a question for which you want an answer, and in case there is any doubt, you quickly change the subject before she could answer. All you want to do is leave a tiny pestering question in her mind that's asking "he doesn't have a date for the dance, yet he didn't even seem to consider me, did he assume I was already asked by someone else? – but he didn't even check."

Then, by dint of careful planning over the previous month or so, you will have scheduled a few lunches with single, attractive women. This is typically only possible for an engineer by pretending to be so busy that he is only free to meet at lunch, by pretending that something is urgent and cannot wait, or whatever. Again, you don't need a sustainable strategy, just a few lunches one week. Of course, these must coincide with Esmeralda's lunches, and of course the other woman must seem to be enjoying them. If necessary, you can create this impression by telling her some good news "hey, we were so impressed by your reco that we've approved your project" which you can then retract by email later. She probably hated you before anyway, so it's not a big loss.

Eventually as the week goes by, Esmeralda starts to wonder why nobody is asking her (because you've knobbled them all) and whether maybe she's slightly underestimated you, and that maybe you have some charm that's beneath the surface and that if these women are willing to be seen with you in public, then maybe it wouldn't be such a disgrace and so on ... So with 2 weeks to go before the event, Esmeralda's payoff matrix looks very different. First of all, her payoff for declining any invitation has gone down, since the risk of not being invited at all suddenly begins to loom. Second, her payoff for accepting to go with you has increased. If you have got everything right, you might just have got to the point where you have a 50/50 chance of being accepted, i.e. something like:

Strategies	*Esmeralda accepts*	*Esmeralda declines*
You invite Esmeralda	*(5,2)*	*(0,2)*
Suitor A asks her	*(1,4)*	*(3,2)*
Suitor B asks her	*(1,2)*	*(3,2)*
Etc ..		

---

[52] Hopefully she won't check and discover that you actually went along alone and hung out with a balding 55-year-old janitor who wasn't able to get a date either ...

At this point, comes the second big problem – how to actually invite Esmeralda without ruining your cool image of not being interested in her as a potential date and having lots of other possibilities. We leave this as an exercise for the student.

In summary, this chapter has provided a very brief introduction to game theory as a way to take advantage of your superior analytical skills to slightly increase your chances of succeeding with women, even when other, normal, men are also interested. We recommend that interested readers consult any of the many good text books on Game Theory for a fuller analysis.

One final caveat to this material is that it has been experimentally confirmed repeatedly that the approaches outlined in the chapter absolutely do not work. For reasons beyond the scope of this text, women are able to play games with men's minds at will, while any attempts men might make to do the same to them come across as immediately transparent, pathetic and laughable to them.

So, should you meet an Esmeralda while studying this chapter, our honest advice would be to just ask her out. Of course she will say no, but you will avoid ruining friendships with co-workers and reducing the company's productivity by 50%.

Chapter 13 My Cup Runneth Over: Management of Multiple Dating Situations

After the distressing, depressing analyses of the previous chapters, in this chapter we look at an altogether more optimistic topic, albeit one which is highly unlikely to be an issue for you personally.

In this context, it's useful to take inspiration from Prof. Stephen Hawking. Among other things, he is famous for having proved that Black Holes can emit radiation (which he even managed to have named after himself) and therefore will eventually evaporate away. The practical effect of this is somewhat limited, in the sense that the typical black hole will evaporate after about 50 billion times the current age of the universe.

But not satisfied with this, he has more recently shown that after this time, the information from the black hole can be recovered.

So, if ever you lose some important information into a black hole, you can be reassured that by waiting about for about 50 billion times the age of the universe, eventually you can get that information back, assuming you're clever enough to understand Prof. Hawking's analysis and you know how to interpret the information coming from the black hole radiation.

It might not sound particularly reassuring the next time that slip of paper with that woman's phone number on it slips into the nearest black hole. But at least you know that theoretically you can find it again.[53]

---

[53] One watchout here is that she will probably have had time to change her number by then – indeed she will probably have changed it the moment she sobered up after giving it to you, that is, in the unlikely event that number she gave you isn't actually that of the permanent undersecretary of the Chinese Communist Party in Beijing.

It is in this frame of mind that you should read this chapter. Are you likely to have to deal with more than one woman who's willing to date you at a single time? Undoubtedly not. But at least you know that the theoretical mechanism exists to deal with this infinitely improbable situation.

The theoretical basis for this analysis was first derived by Bohr, who as his name suggests, was not viewed as a particularly interesting conversationalist, at least by the ladies. While he and Heisenberg strolled the streets of Copenhagen and gazed at the wonderful Danish girls cycling past them, they were inspired to begin a quest for a theoretical approach to meeting some of these girls.

Heisenberg's approach is already well known. His uncertainty principle proved that it's impossible define both the position and the mass of anything, including therefore a woman, with total precision. Therefore, if it were possible to know her weight accurately, there would be a theoretically non-zero uncertainty in her position, which would lead to a much smaller but still non-zero probability that her position could be in Heisenberg's room. This theory even did away with concerns about the walls and doors through the concept of quantum tunneling. However, the one concern with Heisenberg's approach was that he needed to know the weight of the woman in question to a precision of approximatedly 1 in 10^{60} part of the weight of the electron, while practical experiments told him that women when asked their weight either punched him or underestimated their weight by an average of 10^{20} electron masses or more, meaning that the probability of their appearing in his room was less than 1 in 10^{80}, which, he judged, was so low that it wasn't even worth staying in his room just in case.

Bohr's approach was more optimistic. There are two key strands to his approach:

1. The Copenhagen Interpretation involved accepting several apparently nonsensical assumptions, such as Schrödinger example, that a cat in a box with some poison is in an intermediate state between being alive and being dead until somebody checks to see if he's eaten the poison. The key progress here was in the direction of helping people to realise that things aren't always what they seem, and that apparently impossible and illogical situations can and do correspond to reality. It was a simple step from this to his unpublished second paper[54] on the Copenhagen interpretation in which he demonstrated that there was nothing

---

[54] ref. Bohr, N., "Interpretations with Copenhagen women" (unpublished, private correspondence with Bohr estate).

inherently impossible about the concept of a physicist[55] meeting a woman in Copenhagen. This paper was widely circulated in draft form, and was said to be the most important impetus behind the arrival of many post-docs and theoreticians in Copenhagen to work with Bohr on his quantum theory. Only a formal protest by the Women's Institute of Copenhagen prevented the paper's publication and so preserved some of the city's charm for later generations.

2. Bohr then optimistically, although without experimental proof, assumed that attracting women would not be a problem, and set out to define a model of how many women he could handle at a given time. Being a physicist, his interest wasn't so much in keeping them happy or satisfied, but just with keeping them. He was surprised to learn that it was not actually possible to keep an infinite number of women, or more precisely stated, that both the control and intimacy which he could achieve decreased as the number of women increased.

It is now well known that there are several different attractive forces in nature, including the weak and strong nuclear forces, electromagnetism and gravitation. However, at the time of Bohr's work, the nature of the strong nuclear force was not well understood – and he realised that the gravitational model of attraction was a potentially dangerous approach following on from Heisenberg's experiences with asking women their weight. So he decided to focus on the simplest and strongest attraction of which he was aware at the time, the attraction between positive and negative charges.

With the type of sexist analysis which has dominated the scientific literature for hundreds of years, and which also prevails throughout this book, Bohr concluded that the only rational solutions would be those with the male as positive and the female as negative.[56] With this in mind, it was clear that the appropriate model to analyse the multiple-dating situation was the model of

---

[55] Unfortunately the analysis fails for engineers, due to certain unfavourable parameters being knowable with absolute certainty – some of this material is covered in Chapter 4.

[56] It is not fair to consider this as wholly sexist - at the time, cultural anthropologists were aware of some societies in which men took more than one wife, but none in which women took more than one husband. Critics of his conclusion have pointed out that this was not actually an attraction-driven situation – most women didn't want more than one husband – but Bohr appears to have ignored all criticism, and to have based his "proof" on the negativity of the responses he and other physicists received whenever they approached women. .

the atom, in which negatively-charged electrons orbit a positively charged nucleus.

By looking at the atomic model in terms of women surrounding a man, Bohr was immediately able to grasp that this was a seriously unstable situation – any one woman getting too close would spark jealous reactions from the others, which would create an electrically unstable atom[57]. After months of (unfortunately for him) purely theoretical analysis, Bohr finally discovered a solution to this problem. Since his analysis has had important influence on the development of science in the 20th century, it is worth considering in more detail, and this is the subject of the next chapter.

The Bohr Model of Multiple Dating Relationships

There is an old saying that "success breeds success." Just as this is true in business or sport or in practically any other field, it is also true in dating. The irony is that the best way to get a girlfriend is to already have a girlfriend. It is a self-perpetuating cycle of virtuosity. Of course the corollary is that if you aren't part of the scheme, then you are left to your own devices, such as buying this book.

It is also known that the world is full of improbable events, for example a high school dropout inventing the theory of relativity or a former male cheerleader at Yale being elected the president of the United States... twice. So given that thousands, if not millions of people will be reading this book, there is a distinct possibility that one or more of you will be highly successful employing the techniques described in this book and end up having some dates. Perhaps at some point, you will even have a girlfriend. If this occurs it will become obvious to you that your attractiveness level to the opposite sex will be significantly increased. There are a few reasons to explain this "mobbing" phenomenon:

1) You are getting better: By virtue of experience and more contact with the opposite sex, your inherent skills are increasing. You present yourself better, know how to dress better, and are generally becoming more suave and sophisticated. You may even smell better. But don't kid yourself. The actual impact of this self-improvement on your attractiveness is a fairly negligible factor.

2) The seal of approval: Just as we buy products endorsed or approved by various organisations (Good Housekeeping, Underwriters Lab), or

---

[57] we leave it to the reader to investigate how this helps explain the enormous potential for damage, death and destruction of unstable atoms, when used in atomic and nuclear weapons.

recommended by friends, women often choose their partners by means of third party testing. And what better endorsement for a man than the fact that another woman has found that man attractive? The fact that the other woman might be a roommate, friend, sister or co-worker is usually immaterial. It is the stamp of approval which proves one is dateable. Although several engineering organizations[58] have attempted to create standards in this regard, they have generally not been accepted by the female community. For example, the recent ISO certification of datability of a group of male engineers in Norway has not led to increased dating activity of the test group.

3) Competition: The theory goes that women are generally social beings who communicate well and have a nurturing nature and want to get along with everyone. Though this ideal may have some truth, when it comes to mate selection, competition among women is as vicious as on any football field (except the part where they punch each other's nuts in the pile-ups). This behaviour is understandable—for women, going after a "popular" guy is a single-elimination tournament where the winner takes all. In this case, the man is objectified, simply the prize of whatever woman wins the competition. Of course, when one of the women finally does win, it usually results in a severe case of buyer's remorse, but that will be dealt in our chapter titled "Marriage, is it necessarily the end of happiness?"

Whatever the reasons for the phenomenon, it may turn out that you will end up in a multiple dating situation. What does that mean exactly? It is the circumstance in which the engineer has more than one woman interested in him. Okay, let's repeat that: the situation is that the engineer has more than one woman interested in him. This may sound terribly unlikely, but it did actually happen to one of the authors for a period of a few nanoseconds about 15 years ago. Given that experience, we believe that this topic is worth addressing.

While being in a multiple dating situation may sound terrific, it is actually a bewildering feeling, like being invited to be a star in a big budget adult movie. With the rarity of its occurrence, few sources of guidance are available to the average engineer; the rational and structured engineer simply does not have tools to respond to this highly unusual situation. The historical result has been confusion followed by wanton and immoral behaviour of which the rest of us are highly envious. However, the instinctive reaction (hey I can get off with lots of women at the same

---

[58] See ISO TS Standard 117427: Technical Standard: First Ed. Nov 12, 2001 Male Suitability for Partnership: Part 1/A Test for Dimensional Compatability, or DIN Standard 56628, 4A/462, Mar 4, 2003: Testmethode für Weiblicheattraktivitätsgrad, or the somewhat controversial ASTM91143 Test Method for Male Suitability for Reproduction: Hardness and Abrasion Resistance.

time!), in most instances ends very badly, resulting in long periods where feeling are hurt, relationships are broken off, and most importantly, the engineer does not have sex. The key is to develop a system that combines ethical responsibility with the potential of sustainable sex (with partners of choice). We aim in this chapter to use a highly intuitive approach to model optimal responses to this situation.

The framework was developed in 1913 by Niels Bohr, the Danish scientist, who was apparently quite a partying guy (you know those Scandinavians, especially when they're on vacation). As most of you who didn't sleep entirely through freshman chemistry know, Bohr came up with a structure describing atoms, with a nucleus surrounded by electrons, the electrons being in orbits further and further from the nucleus, with the outer orbits able to hold more electrons than the inner ones (see Figure 13.1). At the time it was a brilliant achievement, as it elegantly described atomic phenomena such as light emission and absorption. Bohr won the Nobel prize in 1922 and was then able to score a lot more chicks[59]. Although this model was later proven to be largely incorrect, Bohr will be most remembered for his enduring contribution in multiple dating situations.

Figure 13.1 Bohr Atomic Model

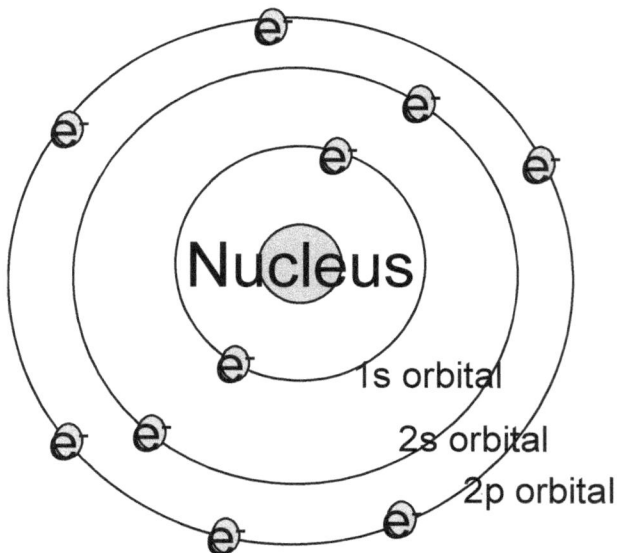

---

[59] This will be addressed in our forthcoming volume, "Scoring Chicks through Groundbreaking Advances in Science".

As Bohr's model goes, the orbitals close to the nucleus can be occupied by fewer electrons, those farther away, by more. We all learned at some point the orbits like *1s2 2s2 2p6 3s2 3p6 3d10*, or however it goes.

With that exciting description, most of you are wondering what the connection of the Bohr atomic model is to multiple dating situations, or are even more likely trying to remember if you even took chemistry at all. The connection is quite straightforward:

You, the engineer, are the nucleus, around which everything revolves. Just as a positively charged nucleus has a bunch of electrons around it, an attractive guy may be surrounded by several women. As the model goes, women, analogous to electrons, are in orbit around you, as shown in Figure 13.2. What is important is that they should be classified into different orbits. For example, in the closest, lowest energy orbitals, you can have two electrons. This orbital we would classify as fairly intimate, that is you are doing the hokey-pokey. Importantly, there should be few in that orbital, (two, according to Niels Bohr, also a well known bigamist).

At higher orbital numbers, say 2, you can have 8 electrons. This second orbital would correspond to women you would go out with on movies, dinners, perhaps with some minor lip contact. The third orbital, with 18 electrons, corresponds to women who are "just friends" that is women usually not seen on a one to one basis. Or these are the ones ending a date with a handshake.

Figure 13.2 Multiple Dating Model

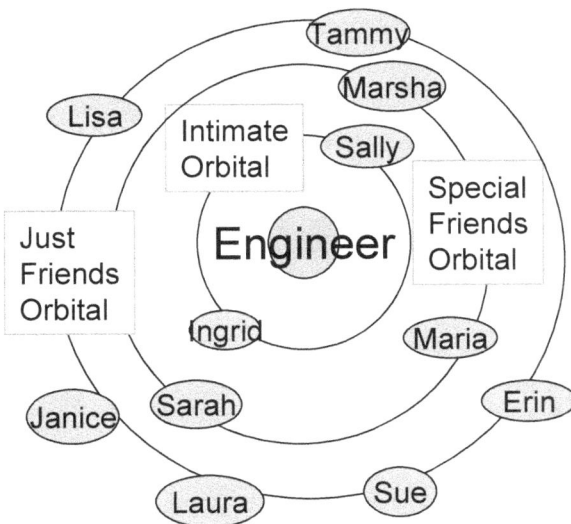

It is worth noting, however, not that we would approve of course, that if there are women in the outer orbitals with whom an occasional intimate encounter would be desirable ("friends with benefits"), it is best that these women reside in the spherical *s*-orbitals, in which they have a significantly higher probability of being momentarily close to the nucleus than do those electrons in the non-spherical orbitals.

According to Bohr, the higher the atomic number, the more orbitals are occupied by electrons. The analogy goes that musicians are more like osmium, whereas engineers are (usually) like hydrogen ions. In the ideal multiple dating scenario, you are at least as far down the periodic table as potassium, with lots of electrons around you. Figures 13.3A and 3B show the difference between a popular guy (like you will be after you finish this book) and an unpopular guy, who has only a few women in remote orbit around him.

Figure 13.3A Popular Guy Orbitals   Figure 13.3B Unpopular Guy Orbitals

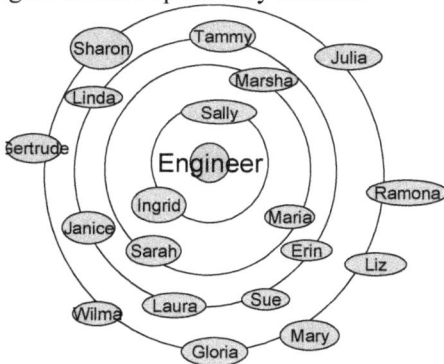

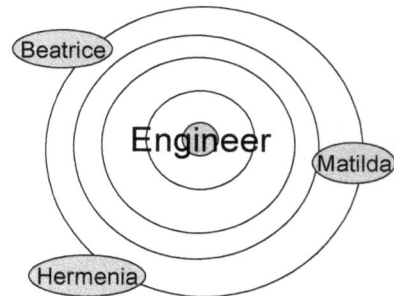

The model also indicates that although the orbital structure remains unchanged, individual electrons may change orbits, being promoted or demoted from one shell to another. This corresponds to the normal flux of intimacy. In Figure 3, we show what happens if Ingrid gives you a well recited "let's just be friends" talk. It is clear that she is moving from the first orbital to a higher orbital, perhaps 2 or 3, or perhaps she will be ejected from the atom altogether. At the same time, it could be that you have a casual acquaintance whom you might happen to see at a party, you both get drunk and something very good happens. As shown in the figure, Linda springs to an inner orbital, which may or may not be what was intended.

As a model, it also indicates certain behaviours that should and should not be exercised. For example, it is not recommended that you be in a regular sleeping relationship with more than 2 women simultaneously. It is forbidden by the quantum mechanical rules, and also pisses off other guys, not to mention at least one if not both women.

Figure 13.4 Orbital Switching

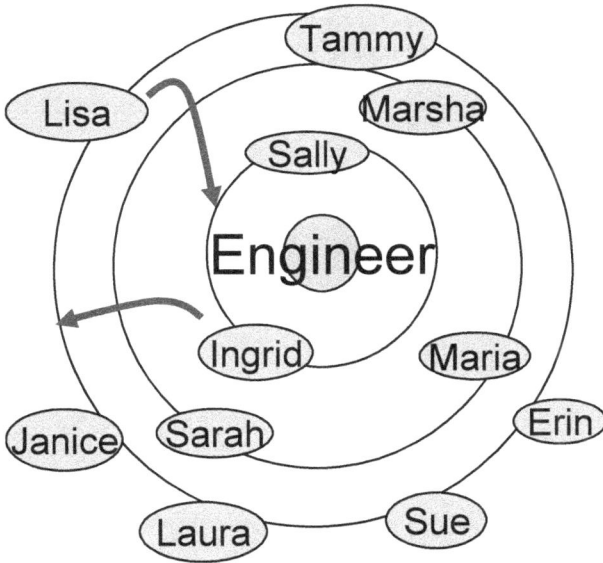

The major damper is the Pauli exclusion principal. Pauli, who was high strung Austrian, and fairly puritanical, proved that two electrons cannot occupy the same space at the same time. This of course means that two women you are seeing should not occupy the same space and same time, unless you are unlucky, or very very very lucky. Although the French and the porn industry would like you to believe otherwise, the number of instances where the exclusion principle is violated is very rare[60].

The analogy goes further when interactions between atoms take place. In this case, when two atoms/nuclei get together – male bonding - it can often happen that electrons are exchanged or promoted and demoted

---

[60] The number of *ménage à trois* incidents is highly exaggerated. In fact it is a mistranslation from French of the phrase *"mèlange à fraises"*, which is apparently some a strawberry dessert, which most French men delight in much more than sex. However, see the analysis of the logical possibility of a threesome with beautiful twins in the footnotes referring to Bertrand Russell's philosophy above (Ch 6).

within orbitals. Ionic bonding, the transfer of electrons from one atomic sphere to another is akin to introducing a woman that you know to a friend of yours, a fairly common occurrence. Transfer of electrons from the inner orbitals is less likely as they are more tightly held—similarly the phenomenon of engineers stealing each others girlfriends is fairly rare. Also, the circumstance of covalent bonding, that is where electrons are shared between nuclei, is fairly rare, except in California.[61]

Ultimately this model is only a guideline, but fighting it is fighting against all the little atoms that make up your body. It will also make your life easier if you follow the quantum mechanical rules.

Table 13-1

Shell	Orbitals	Number of electrons / women	Sphere of Intimacy
1	*1s(2)*	*2*	*Intimate*
2	*2s(2) 2p(6)*	*8*	*Casual dating*
3	*3s(2) 3p(6) 3d(10)*	*18*	*Friends*
4	*4s(2) 4p(6) 4d(10) 4f...*	*...*	*Acquainted*

---

[61] And apparently France: interested readers might like to consult the recent French bestseller "The sexual life of Catherine M" – maybe there's something about strawberries .. (Ed.)

Chapter 14 Sex – The Cantilever Model

This is going to be where most of you browsing the book in a bookstore will first turn looking for pictures of naked women or at least women crawling all over engineers. Sorry. (we did look but couldn't find any)

As is well known, there are two ways to look at sex. While each has its strong adherents[62], we feel that the two approaches can be complementary, and that an engineer who can master both (on a theoretical level at least) will be well served in the unlikely event he should get the opportunity to put this learning into practice.

The first approach, which we study in this chapter, deals with the so-called differential model of sex, first outlined by Professor Hanratty of Princeton in his classic 1961 paper, "Sex", published in the *Abstracts of the Physical Sciences,* Vol 25 – surprisingly, this issue had the highest sales of any issue of that review.

In the next chapter, we shall consider the more modern hydrodynamical approach to sex – which, while clearly more sophisticated, has been considered by some to lack the necessary rigidity, so to speak.

Sex

Whether actually enjoyable or not, sex is the ultimate payoff for all of the previous work. Sex is certainly one of the main objectives of the dating activity. It represents more than physical intimacy and satisfaction.

---

[62] Readers may recall the minor fracas at the *AIChE* conference in Miami in 1974 when Prof. Sweeney of Illinois interrupted a presentation by Dr. J Fresno of Michigan to challenge his competence to talk about sex at all, given his limited understanding of fluid mechanics.

It is a deliverable, a concrete result, evidence that you have been at least relatively successful at dating. It is like an A on a midterm, just a little more sweaty.

Much has been written about sex, but most of it is really too diffuse to be useful to the average engineer. The so called classics in this area, such as the *Joy of Sex* or the *Kama Sutra*, focus primarily on the more holistic aspects of the subject and are entirely lacking in engineering rigor. Generally, one sees pictures of two individuals with limbs in highly contorted positions with no definitions of the critical angles, dimensions or equations of motion. These vague descriptions are then interspersed with gibberish about aspects such as feelings, emotions and so on, which only cloud the picture.

So it is clear that a more concrete formulation is necessary. The diagram on the following page gives a detailed engineering guide to sex. In case it's still not clear, here is a description of what the diagram signifies:

Body A pivots about point m with frequency ω, circumscribing an angle θ. Body A is connected to part B at point n. Member C is connected to body B at point o. Body B is also connected to part D at point q. Part D is generally fixed, except able to rotate at point r, which is tangent to the ground.

The pivoting of body A causes body B to oscillate along line L. The equation describing the motion of body B is a function of θ and ω, with its exact formulation left as an exercise for the reader.

The motion of body B likewise causes motion of member C along line L. Since the point of attachment o is rigid, the displacement of C, equals that of B, namely plus minus δ. Note that C has a significant elongation at break, roughly 300%. C should also have a Young's modulus exceeding 11.1 GPa[63], alternative standards define a minimum Rockwell hardness (ASTM D785) of R25. In no cases should C be allowed to deflect beyond more than 30%, otherwise you will have to see a physician.

An important complication is that the Young's modulus of member C varies highly by individual and age, as well as the characteristics of body M. If the properties of C do not meet the above specifications, there are a variety of mechanical and pharmaceutical methods, widely advertised by reputable internet commerce providers, which may improve mechanical properties. Despite well accepted success in other cantilever applications, methods employing the use of composite elements, including epoxy, carbon fiber and metallic reinforcement are not recommended[64].

---

[63] A value of 11.1 GPa is typical for Black Spruce Wood, hence the origin of the term "woody".

[64] Puck A.; *Zur Beanspruchung und Verformung von GFK-Mehrschichtverbunden-Bauelementen*, Kunstoffe, Vol. 57, Heft 4-7, 1967.

At the correct time point, which will be explained by the body M, member C should be inserted into slot N, with point *f* being the point of entry. For best results, member C, in particular point *p*, should reach point G in body M. Contact between member C and point *f* has also shown to be important.

Studies have shown that the optimal δ is in the range of 50 to 150 mm, which significantly depends on the length of member C. In no case should delta exceed the length of member C, as then the process must be started over.

Use of friction reducing materials in the range of 1000 cp to 10,000 cp, and preferably Mw in the range of 10,000, has been shown to reduce the friction factor *f*, thereby allowing higher frequency levels ω to be achieved.

The length of member C is not as important as that body M be respected in the morning.[65]

If body M is not well known, it is highly advised that member C be sheathed in an elastic material, preferably a crosslinked natural or synthetic latex of thickness between 0.2 and 0.5 mm. The elastic material should have a permeability not exceeding 1.5×10^{-8} m^2/hr. The elastic material may also be patterned or formed from materials in attractive colours such as Ferrari Red, navy Blue or fluorescent orange.

The oscillation process begins with ω at lower values (0.3 Hz) followed by increasing omega and θ at values up to 1 Hz and 45 degrees respectively.

At some point member C will experience a sudden loss in Young's modulus. At that point, the process is terminated and you may roll over and go to sleep.

The main thing to remember is not to make it too mechanical.

---

[65] Allegedly.

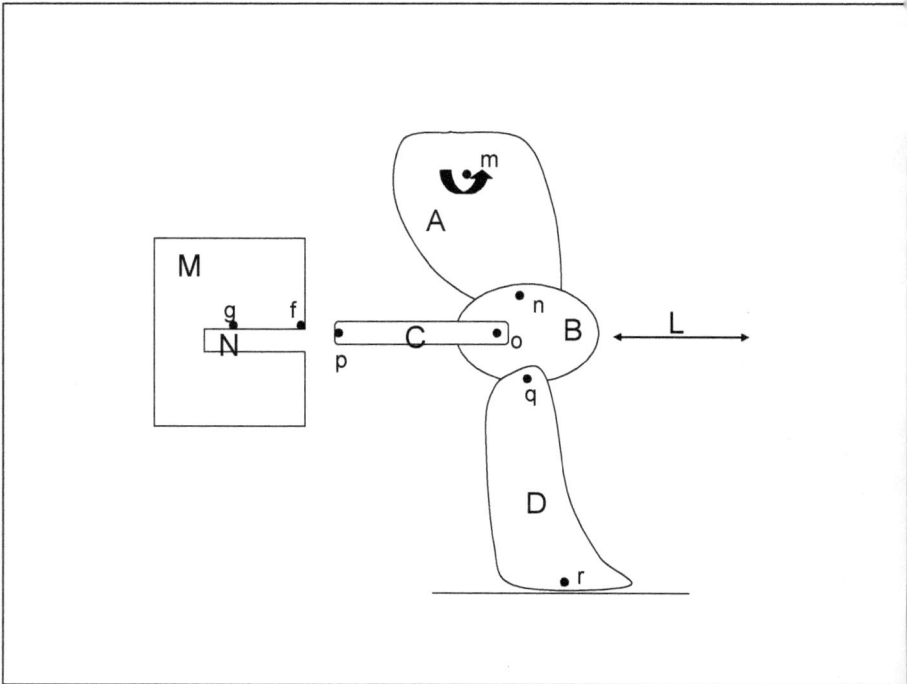

Figure 14.1 A gentleman making love to a lady – diagrammatic representation

Chapter 15   Sex: The Macromolecularhydrodynamical Model

"The act of sexual intercourse essentially involves the transfer of approximately 1 ml of a non-Newtonian fluid along a long, narrow, flexible cavity."

John W. Scale, ChE Faculty, U. Of Michigan, 1982[66]

This chapter deals with the fluid-dynamical model of sex, sometimes also referred to as the macromolecularhydrodynamical model, in recognition of the non-Newtonian quality of several of the fluids involved[67], and also of the fact that, since Newton died a virgin, anyone practicing this technique is inherently behaving in a non-Newtonian manner, much in the manner of someone not sitting under an apple tree.

Viewed as described by Prof. Scale, above, the concept seems remarkably simple, and indeed once this idea has been grasped, it truly becomes mystifying why so many books have been written about such a simple topic. However, many Chemical Engineers have been misled to view the topic as more difficult than it actually is through the

---

[66] Tragically, Prof. Scale died from boredom during a faculty seminar on Process Control. He left no descendents.

[67] A non-Newtonian fluid is typically a polymeric liquid whose effective viscosity varies with flowrate – or more specifically, with shear-rate – on a microscopic scale, this results from the "stringy" molecules aligning as the flowrate increases, so reducing the internal friction. Frequently, non-Newtonian fluids also have a "yield stress" – a minimal stress below which the fluid does not flow at all – as with a bottle of ketchup which doesn't flow until you hit the bottom of the bottle.

understandable error that the most logical place to look for information about sex would be in their lecture notes on "fluid flow in packed beds".[68]

The most natural approach, then, to sex, might appear to be to look at the application of the Poiseuille equation, with the initial simplifying assumption of Newtonian behaviour, and of an approximately circular cross-section.

$$Q = \pi r^4 \Delta P / 8\mu L$$

where obviously the appropriate corrections for the non-Newtonian nature of the fluid could be made either by the assumption of a simple model (e.g. power law, with the effective viscosity given by $\eta = K(\gamma')^n$) or by calculating the flowrate computationally using experimental rheology data.

However, this approach has been shown not to function due to the somewhat frustrating nature of the cavity in question, namely the elastic properties of the walls which cause it to close to radius 0 unless it is maintained open by the use of a mechanical device of some kind. Given the dependence of the flowrate on the fourth power of the radius, this predictably reduces the flowrate to a point where insemination is highly improbable.

The obvious approach there, and that which engaged workers for the 20 years from the Poiseuille analysis, was to design an implement which could be used to transfer the fluid to the other end of the cavity in question – for simplicity, let us imagine each of these designs to have been variants on the theme of a straw, with varying materials of construction, inner and outer diameters, rigidities, lengths and so forth.

While there were certainly merits to this approach, there were also limitations which ultimately resulted in its replacement. These can be grouped into two types:

    1.   Lack of adequate pressure differential and/or inadequate fluid quantities. These closely related problems stem from the fact that the quantity of fluid available is typically 1 ml or less. In order to maintain a pressure differential, the tube needs to be filled, so we are left with the inequality $\pi r^2 L < 1$ ml. For the shortest acceptable

---

[68] Indeed, it has been claimed that an efficient model of sex can be derived simply by modelling the flow in a packed-bed and then taking the limit as the voidage increases to a point where the particles in the bed have room to vibrate in the sinusoidal manner described in the previous chapter. Building on this, some researchers have simplified the approach further by taking the limit as the number of particles in the bed approaches 2, but this has been shown experimentally to be an unnecessary simplification. (ref. *Annals of UW Fraternity parties*, Hellenic Press, 1979)

tube length, of approximately 10 cm, this means that the tube radius needs to be less than about 1.8 mm. Given the high viscosity of the fluid, as the equation above suggests, the pressure differential required to generate a significant flowrate in a tube this narrow is several orders of magnitude beyond what has been observed to be generated experimentally.[69]

2. Entry difficulties. It was repeatedly observed in experiments that men, both engineers and non-engineers, had difficulty achieving the necessary precision required to inject the fluid into a narrow tube. Even where time was taken to ensure perfect alignment beforehand, it appeared that at the moment of ejaculation, for reasons which have not been fully understood, experimental subjects momentarily lost the ability to focus and to aim precisely. While this could be overcome by the use of a funnel type entrance, this resulted only in even more serious pressure drop issues.

Having concluded that a hollow tube did not seem to work, one of the most famous scientific experiments of the 20th century was carried out. Could the answer be a non-hollow tube? The experiment was carried out using a cigar. An apparently illogical choice, in that one would expect very little fluid to pass through a cigar other than perhaps by a very slow process of diffusion or osmosis. And initial results were not very encouraging, in that the fluid was observed to not so much flow through the cigar as to be directed onto the clothing of the female volunteer.

However, much to the surprise of the scientific community, a very high-level analysis of this experiment concluded, albeit without unanimity, that sexual intercourse had actually taken place.

For a time it was believed that this might be the solution to the problem, and indeed the Cuban economy received a considerable boost due to increased cigar sales. However, in communities where this form of sexual intercourse was practiced exclusively, it was found that the number of births dropped dramatically, with the population only being maintained through the influx of dry-cleaners from other areas. This prompted further study which suggested that, in fact, while this technique may formally satisfy the US Senate definition of sexual intercourse, it fails to satisfy the more natural definition, namely that of potentially impregnating the female.

---

[69] While direct measurements of actual pressure are difficult, it is possible to back-calculate by analysing the trajectory – this matter is not considered appropriate for this text, but those interested in further background reading on this matter might like to consult some of the analyses of Drs. Peter Cook and Dudley Moore in their *Derek & Clive* series.

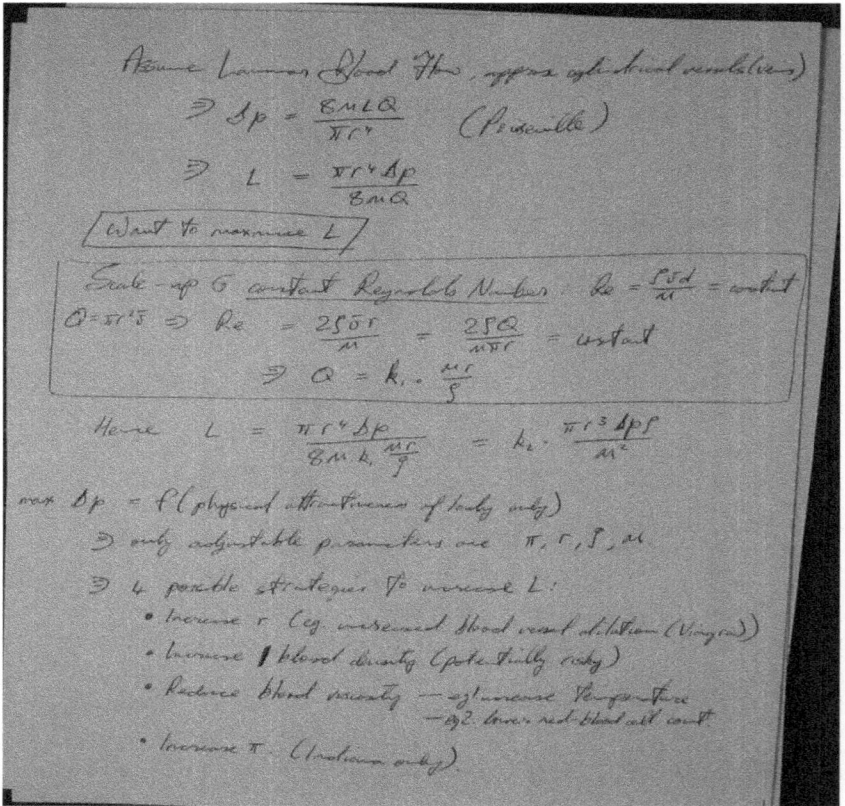

Figure 15.1 You may think that all the junk mail you receive about "how to gain an extra 2 inches" is a new phenomenon. But in fact this has long been an area of interest to engineers with feelings of inadequacy ... and it has prompted some excellent analyses, and also some very poor ones, of which the above is a classic example from the early 1950's. Post-doctoral student George Dukakis used this analysis to convince fellow-student Pete Maguire that increasing the density or decreasing the viscosity of his blood would effectively lengthen his penis during intercourse. He also may have inadvertently invented Viagra, but did not realise the opportunity.

Experimental studies (which failed to attract female participants, unfortunately) showed that the theory was flawed – while at the same time showing why Indiana men really would have had longer penises than anyone else if their legislature had agreed to a 1897 proposal to set the value of $\pi = 4$.

Clearly a totally new approach was needed, and it is at this point that a fortuitous interaction took place at a conference on non-Newtonian fluid mechanics in Chicago, between some leading workers in the macromolecularhydrodynamical modelling of sex, and a modest Indian post-grad student. Observing the student's apparent irresistibility to the female conference attendees, one of the researchers asked why this was, and learned that the student was renowned as a master in the art of sexual techniques.

The researchers quickly arranged for an interview with the student, who modestly chooses to remain anonymous[70], and were amazed to learn of an already extensive literature in the field of sexual technique, going back for many centuries. They were preparing themselves for several months of reading articles and piecing together the theory, but the student informed them that there was in fact one short book which contained all the most important learnings, and indeed, since he himself had long ago memorised the text, he was happy to sell them his copy for a relatively modest fee.

On reading the text, the researchers were amazed to discover a totally innovative idea. To overcome the difficulty of transferring the fluid into the end of the cavity, they Indians had discovered the remarkable solution inserting the rodlike male appendage directly into the female cavity, and (here was the truly inspired part) by doing this *before* the fluid was ejected by the male. In this way, the fluid was injected directly at the far end of the cavity, thus eliminating the need for the Poiseuille analysis and indeed eliminating all issues related to the high "viscosity" of the fluid.

At first it seemed that the definitive solution had been found, and that finally mankind would be able to reproduce freely. However, it proved to be not quite so simple. Indeed this new technique brought new fluid-dynamical challenges, due to the need to reduce the friction between the rod and the cavity. Experiments and anecdotal evidence from colleagues' experiences (with their wives and girlfriends) has confirmed that the cavity is typically very dry, and therefore in need of lubrication.[71]

Disturbingly for those who choose to believe in either evolution or an intelligent creator, it is found that the process as recommended by the Indian researchers, while otherwise coherent, involves the release of the

---

[70] His name is Rustam …

[71] One female colleague claimed that there exists some supernatural process by which the cavity can be caused to self-lubricate, involving something she referred to as "four play". Involving two additional people seemed somewhat inefficient, and also somewhat inappropriate at what is, after all, a relatively private moment for both partners, and so we believe that the approach derived here does offer practical benefits in convenience, cost and speed.

fluid into the cavity only after significant frictional forces due to the forward and backward motion of the rod within the cavity have been overcome. How much easier it would be if some of the fluid could be released in time to be used as a lubricant – however, those who have tried this have found that the Young's modulus of the rod (a critical parameter, as discussed in the previous chapter) decreases suddenly, to the point where even the added lubrication no longer allows the frictional forces to be overcome. Clearly a design flaw, but one that we as engineers need to overcome.

In short, the Indian technique solves one macromolecularfluiddynamical problem, that of flow of a viscous fluid, only to replace it with another, that of finding an appropriate fluid to appreciably reduce the frictional forces between two solid bodies in rapid motion.

Fortunately, the second problem is significantly less challenging than the first, and having carefully studied the properties that this fluid would need to have, researchers were fortunate to discover that an appropriate fluid had not only been designed, but had been used even in the context of sexual relations for several years. The fluid in question was a mix of high-molecular-weight hydrocarbons, with a yellowish, greasy appearance, sold in many countries under trade names such as *Vaseline*®. Indeed, it was found that many married couples with young children had for years considered this essential for sexual intercourse, applying it liberally on the door-handle to prevent the children entering the room.

It was only a short matter of time, during which extensive validation work was carried out, before it was confirmed that it would be appropriate to test the same fluid for use as a lubricant. After mixed initial results, some fine-tuning of the fluid led to the availability of some excellent anti-frictional products, widely available today in tubes that resemble (but ideally should not be confused with) toothpaste.

Thus was solved the challenge so eloquently defined by Prof. Scale at the start of this chapter. But that is not to say that the researchers are resting on their laurels. The process is still considered highly energy-intensive and, frankly, too sweaty. It is hoped that in the next few years, a process will be devised which will avoid all this unpleasantness and inefficiency. Indeed, Prof. Scale, now retired but still actively following the latest developments and in close contact with some of the leading workers in the field[72], envisages the day in the not too distant future when "a man will be able to go out on a Saturday afternoon for a quiet game of golf, leaving his good lady wife at home embroidering some cushion

---

[72] It appears that the news of Prof. Scale's untimely death, communicated earlier in the chapter, may have been somewhat premature. We apologise for any distress this may have caused to his family and friends.

covers, and come home from his game of golf to find that the work of insemination of his wife has been completed in his absence, without any undue effort or perspiration on either side."[73]

---

[73] He hastened to point out that he did not wish this idea to be confused with the already existing technique described by James Joyce in his classic treatise, *Ulysses*, in which the insemination was carried out by a third party.

Section E:

Preparing for the Unexpected

What To Do in Case You're Successful

Chapter 16: Stopping While You're (as far) Ahead (as possible)

Eventually (so the theory goes), you will tire of dating a different beautiful woman every couple of weeks, and you'll begin to think about settling down with just one partner. This chapter does not enter into any discussion on the wisdom of such a decision, or the reasons why you might be tempted to take a decision that so obviously flies in the face of everything that common sense or evolutionary biology has taught you[74]. We don't even care whether your partner of choice is likely to be male, female, ovine or Minnesotan. We focus exclusively on the mathematics you'll need to decide when you've met a partner who is statistically about as good[75] as you're likely to get.

Other authors on this subject would talk about love or feeling right and other vague, non-mathematical concepts, but a true engineer would never resort to such a non-reproducible decision method, based on unquantifiable and unreliable data. On which point is should be noted that much scientific research shows that being in love is anyhow a state of temporary insanity in terms of brain chemistry, and even the non-mathematicians suggest that it's no appropriate state in which to take life-altering decisions.[76]

---

[74] You might also want to read the following chapter.

[75] Again, we stress that "good" in this context is used as a purely relative concept, in the sense for example that a 30-year-old male engineer who liked young women with teeth might consider a 70-year-old with two-teeth to be better (more good) than a 75-year-old with one tooth.

[76] cf. also Paradise by the Dashboard Light, from *Bat out of Hell*, by Meat Loaf.

So the reality is that for most non-engineers, there is no reliable way to decide if the partner you're in love (or lust) with is the appropriate life-partner, other than waiting until you're not in love anymore, which frankly would take some of the fun out of the whole thing. But by following the techniques presented here, you will be able to avoid any risks of taking a decision that you'll regret later.[77]

So, how do you know if you've found the right person to settle down with? For many a non-engineer, this is not typically a decision which would be taken through a detailed mathematical analysis at all. To give one example, many people settle when they believe they have found their dream partner. How do they decide this? They make a comparison between their actual partner and the type of partner they dream about. Sounds simple.

However, not for engineers. Engineers dream about tripling the capacity of a silicon chip with one brilliant idea, or being able to spend a whole day tinkering with their car engine. And while these are valid dreams *per se*, they do not provide the type of detailed information about the ideal partner which is so key to taking the correct decision on whether a particular person is the one for life.

It's a common fallacy that maybe these dreams are telling us that our ideal partner would be someone who also likes tinkering with the car engine all day, but a quick Einsteinian thought-experiment can disprove this: Imagine it's Sunday, and the car is outside in the driveway. Imagine further that you have found a perfect partner who likes nothing better than to tinker with a car-engine all day. As indeed do you. The result: unless it's a very very big engine like a 64 Dodge Dart, it's going to be tough for both of you to even have access to the engine, and undoubtedly each of your tinkering is going to counteract the tinkering of the partner – leading to a thoroughly non-ideal situation of two frustrated partners. Moral: beware of following your dreams too literally.

Of course, this concern can be eliminated by choosing the engine itself as the partner. Mathematically and logically, this is an acceptable solution. However, in this case, you will (perhaps) be pleased to discover that, provided you do not choose to formalise your union with the engine in a church[78] or registry office, there is nothing in our social norms which prevents you from choosing another partner (e.g. a woman or a man) *as well*, in which case the following analysis applies to the choice of that

---

[77] With the possible exception of some of the issues highlighted in chapter 17...

[78] If you do plan to formalise the union in a Catholic Church, be aware that typically they will require you both to follow a 6-month pre-marital course to ensure that you are well suited to each other.

second partner – and this process can repeated *ad infinitum* until a partner of the human variety is chosen.

For this reason, in this chapter we provide a framework within which you can take the critical decision of how to identify if the person you're currently with is the best possible partner to settle down with, without having to resort to the randomness of emotional judgments, the chaos of DNA analysis or pheromone theory, or the absurdity of taking such decisions in a state of temporary insanity.

Or if you'd rather skip all the long and largely pointless introduction above, here's a much shorter version: if you're with someone and you're not sure if it's time to settle down and have kids, this chapter will give you the answer.

A brief aside on the necessity of this knowledge. Both men and women, both engineers and non-engineers, achieve different levels of attractiveness as they move through life. While there will be exceptional cases like someone who wins the Lotto on her 75th birthday or an otherwise attractive woman who decided at age 20 to switch from studying Babylonian archeological philosophies to enter Electronic Engineering, in general, for most people, this is a relatively smooth curve. It's true that for the typical engineer, the curve tends to remain rather more close to the $y=0$ axis than it does for the average person, but this is not the subject of this chapter.

In youth (which we'll define as 18 to avoid any legal problems), most of us are still approaching our physical and mental peak. So for a few years we see a very strong positive trend, as we become physically more beautiful, mentally more interesting, and financially more capable of buying decent clothes[79], splurging on soppy gifts and paying for meals.

After a few years of purely positive trend, however, some of the variables begin to change. After leaving university, a lack of physical exercise begins to show its effects on our once apolloesque / venusesque physiques. The first wrinkles begin to appear – even an occasional grey hair. But these initially minor imperfections are at first more than compensated for by our ever growing financial security, increased self-confidence, and in the case of non-engineers, improved social skills. So the curve of our attractiveness continues to rise, just a little more slowly.

After a further time, however, while we may continue to improve in some aspects, the physical degradations, the effect of stress, the outmodedness of our thinking, the fact that most others in our age-group

---

[79] We emphasise "financially" capable here, as even with age, many engineers will never develop the most basic notion of how to dress – as discussed in a previous chapter.

are paired-up and so on, begin to outweigh any positive trends, so that our attractiveness begins to decrease – beginning an accelerating spiral towards death and having our bodies eaten by disgusting insects, at which point our attractiveness can be considered to closely approximate to 0 [80]. Some representative data for US males is shown in the figure below.

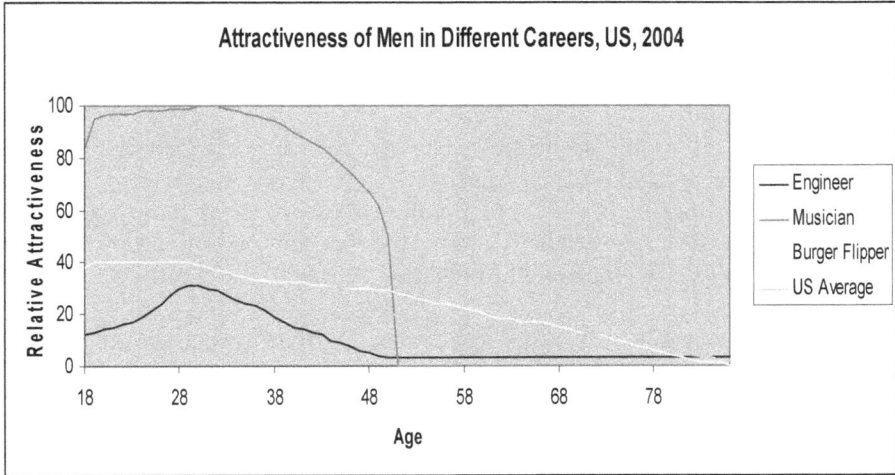

Fig 16.1. Interesting to note is that while Musicians are by far the most attractive up to the age of about 50, their attractiveness suffers a sharp decline. This is due to musicians older than 50 being mostly either dead or Mick Jagger. Those with career growth in their early 20's show some attractiveness growth, but McDonald's employees who fail to advance beyond burger flipping retain their attractiveness longer due to the increasing value of being able to get free food. Senoir men who work in McDonald's are notoriously successful with the elderly ladies who like to sit chatting over a cup of coffee for hours – their favourite customer might get extra sugar one day, a large instead of a medium coffee another day, sometimes even an Egg McMuffin snuck onto her tray when the manager isn't looking. Next thing you know, the manager discovers the pair of them out behind the skip at the back, two half naked 75-year-olds lying among the old burger wrappers and half-eaten fries, their bodies covered in ketchup and flat Coke. [Sorry about that last visual – Ed.]

The key, therefore, is to be able to identify the moment in life when the curve maxes out and begins to drop, and to realise that at that point, or very soon after, it might be wise to stick with the partner you have found

---

[80] Unless attractiveness to electronic engineering post-grad students is considered meaningful.

(assuming the partner is willing, which is a subject beyond the scope of this chapter, but adequately covered in many others).

Of course, this assumes that the partner you've found at your point of maximum attractiveness is necessarily your most attractive partner. This should be true if you've been following the techniques we've outlined in the previous chapters, but to avoid doubt, we will provide techniques for ensuring that this is indeed the case – requiring nothing more than combining the different analyses below.

There are different approaches possible, the choice depending on the available information, the assumptions you're willing to make as to the statistical distribution of the women you're likely to meet, and whether the success criteria relate exclusively to the partner you end up with, or include other factors such as minimisation of the time-delay or pre-nuptial agreements.

In terminology which is likely to be more familiar to you, we're going to offer three basic approaches which in theory might yield the same conclusion:

1. N-dimensional vector analysis combined with simple Gaussian statistics – the kindergarten analysis.
2. N-dimensional vector analysis combined with partial differential equations solution – a bit more mathematically sophisticated.
3. The 99% analysis – a simpler technique that will work in 99% of cases.

Each of the three approaches above focuses exclusively on an analysis of your partner. A fourth analysis technique, as mentioned in the introduction to this chapter, is that of analysing yourself and working out if you are approaching your peak, at your peak, or if you are already on the slippery slope downhill and in desperate need to cling to any out-hanging branch without asking too many questions about it. This leads us to:

4. Self-analysis – differential calculus approach.

Approach 1

Let's first consider the simplest case, with the following assumptions:
*   you have a well-defined time-frame within which you want to find a partner (e.g. 2 years, or if we want to be realistic, 12 years)

- you have read chapter 11, and so are capable of converting the n-dimensional variable describing the appeal of potential candidates into a scalar variable whose value is directly proportional to the candidate's appeal. Let us define the <u>scalar</u> attractiveness variable $A_m(x_{1m}, x_{2m}, \ldots, x_{nm})$, where for each candidate, m, the x_{nm} are independent variables describing her n different attributes. The process of defining and calculating this variable has been described in detail in Chapter 11.

- You have sufficient "experience" both of women and of your capacity to attract them to feel capable of assessing the average value of A_{ave} among likely candidates – i.e. those willing to date you – we're using the plural here purely to boost your morale - assuming obviously that no drastic changes in the quality of potential candidates or in your ability to attract them will occur during the allowed time-period. (Caveat: during this period you will probably lose any hair you have left, gain about 20 kg (44 lbs) and develop some very innovative body odor problems, so this assumption is optimistic).

- Furthermore, you have sufficient experience to be able to map out the variability of candidates in terms of some parameterisable distribution about that average, giving a statistical function (e.g. (but not necessarily) a Gaussian distribution) which can be subjected to normal statistical analyses. Let us define the probability of a candidate having appeal A by the function $p(A)$.

- You can estimate how many likely candidates you will meet in any given period of time – this again being a statistical variable with mean and variation defined based on previous experience. Let us define the probability of having k candidate-meetings in a period t as $r(k;t)$, where clearly if k is approximated as a continuous variable[81], then: $\int_0^\infty r(k;t)\, dk = 1$. This equality will be useful to us in the analysis the follows.

The situation most closely resembles iterative processes in mathematics, or for the older engineers among you, the do-loops in Fortran. At each iteration, there comes a decision point:

Remain with current partner
or
Reenter dating lottery and hope to find "better".

---

[81] Strictly speaking, this should of course be a summation over all integer values of k. However, this renders the math significantly more complex to treat and offers no additional insights.

There are distinct considerations to be taken into account:

1. What is the probability of meeting a "better" candidate within the remaining time period?

To calculate this probability for a given number of meetings, n, you must multiply the probabilities that each of the n encounters will *not* produce a better candidate, and subtract this from *1*. Let's assume that the attractiveness of your current partner is A_c. Since we've assumed that no important changes occur during the time period, then, the probability that you will not meet a better candidate reduces to

$$P = [p(A<A_c)]^n.$$ Eq. 13.1

Where the value, n, is itself a statistical variable, which again, for simplicity we assume to be continuous, although obviously a sum would be more precise. The sum/integral over all values of n is taken, multiplied by the probability function, r.

$$P(t) = \int_0^\infty r(n;t)\ [p(A<A_c)]^n\ dn$$ Eq. 13.2

2. What is the risk of *not* meeting any candidate who meets the minimum requirements (A_{min}) as a suitable partner within the remaining time?

Similarly to Eq. 13.2, this is given by:

$$P(t) = \int_0^\infty r(n;t)\ [p(A<A_{min})]^n\ dn$$ Eq. 13.3

3. Viewed in this way, the problem would appear trivial. However, careful consideration will reveal a flaw in this simplistic logic. Or rather many flaws:

- Since you will live for only a finite number of years, and many of these may well be spent in a state of extreme senility, painful debilitating illnesses or marriage, surely your enjoyment of the finite time of your search should be a relevant consideration. Let us refer to this as the Finite Horizon Problem.
- The simplistic analysis above assumes that this decision process needs to be taken only one time – in reality, it will need to be taken with every partner, after sufficient time has elapsed to allow you to evaluate her accurately. And of course, as each new partner

brings new data to the mix, you will also need to rerun your cluster analysis every time, incorporating the new data. This may theoretically result in you spending more time actually tabulating, correlating and calculating during a given relationship than you spend in the relationship itself, which creates serious philosophical issues at non-relativistic calculation velocities. It may also be seen as somewhat anti-social by your partner, especially as it leaves very little time for foreplay. This is known in the literature as the Holy Grail problem, for obvious reasons"[82]

- The analysis assumes a yes/no answer is possible. However, it's obviously more accurate to think of this in terms of risk analysis. If your starting point is A=73, and you calculate a 58% likelihood of achieving at least A=75 over the next 4 years, with a 27% chance of surpassing A=82, that may seem a worthwhile investment. But obviously your willingness to take this risk would also depend on a careful analysis of what happens if you fail to achieve this, as would be the case in 42% of cases. If you can be 98% sure that you'd finish with at least A=67, that's a very different situation from one in which there's a 13% chance that you'd finish with A=23 at the end of the prescribed time period. So the analysis needs to look not simply at the probability of exceeding your current status, but rather at the full probability function of your likely status after the prescribed time. Predictably enough, Wilson, who first noticed this problem in his classic 1958 thesis "A statistical analysis of the effect of more frequent hair-waxing on the slugging percentage of 25 engineering students", called this the stolen base problem – a reference to the play in baseball which can get you from first to second base ... or can leave you with nothing.

Let us consider each of these problems in turn, although the process is greatly simplified by the fact that a full analysis of the first problem largely addresses the other two as well. While the full philosophical, mathematical and psychological treatment of these is beyond this scope of this book, we will outline in broad strokes how they might be addressed: [Readers who value what little sanity they have left are strongly encouraged to skip this analysis – Ed.]

The Finite Horizon Problem
Essentially the objective here would be to define a variable $E(t)$ which expresses how much you enjoy each moment in a relationship, as a

---

[82] "Sex is more fun than logic. I can't prove it. It just is."

function of the age of the relationship. Philosophers have debated how one might maximise this for centuries. We will follow the Utilitarians in assuming that it is somehow possible to determine or estimate this, and focus only on how this information is then to be used.

We assume, reasonably, that there is a serial correlation relationship[83] between the attractiveness of the partner you end up with and the likely enjoyment you expect to experience in the time you spend together. Of course this cannot be proven, but we have to assume that that is your motivation in defining your attractiveness scale in this way. If you have chosen do define as highly attractive a partner who will make you miserable, that is not our fault.

To simplify the example in a way which in no way invalidates the approach, we assume this correlation to be linear. Furthermore, in line with our previous definition of the minimum attractiveness level acceptable, A_{min}, we define E_{min}, the corresponding enjoyment level, to be the level of enjoyment per unit time in case of remaining single. This is trivially valid if A_{min} has been appropriately defined.

Figure 16.2   This photograph, taken at a new-hires party at a major multinational, highlights one of the major downsides of following the theories outlined in this chapter for those whose mental arithmetic skills are not at the required level. The male engineer (in the middle, for the unitiated) is being accosted by beautiful women, whom he has cleverly convinced that he's a rich heir to the throne of a newly independent East Asian monarchy. However, rather than accept their advances, or propose the famous Bertrand Russell solution of a threesome (see footnotes Chapter 6), he is lost in calculation, trying to work out the complex integral equation in his head to decide whether he really would be wise to

[83] By this, we simply mean, for potential partners i and j, if Ai > Aj, then on average Ei > Ej.

date either of the two. An engineer more practiced in the art of rapid calculation would not face this issue.

Finally, it is necessary to estimate, again with a probability function, how long you will live and how the quality of your life will vary over that time. Let $s(t)$ be the probability that you will be alive at age t, where obviously $\int_{now}^{\infty} (ds/dt)\, dt = -1$, i.e. there is a probability of exactly one that you will die between now and the end of the universe. Immortal beings will have to make the appropriate adjustment to the derivations which follow, as will cats. To avoid unnecessary complication, we will assume an "average" level of good health and average all the other factors too into one variable, $H(t)$, in such a way as it is reflects the average change in enjoyment of life with age, which can reflect, for example, positve changes like retirement, grandchildren, respect, etc., as well as negative changes like ill-health. We will define $H(t)$ in such a way that it directly multiplies the other factors to produce the final enjoyment coefficient.

With this approach, it is now possible to calculate precise expectation values for the total enjoyment[84] for the two choices open to you – namely staying with your partner or re-entering the dating field. In the case of staying with your partner, the calculation is trivially:

$$E_{total} \quad = \quad \int_{now}^{\infty} s(t).H(t).E_c\,(t-t_s)dt \qquad\qquad \text{Eq. 13.4}$$

where E_c is the enjoyment expectation with your current partner, of attractiveness A_c, and t_s is the time when the relationship with your current partner started.

The corresponding calculation for leaving your partner and re-entering the dating world is logically equally straightforward, but much more complicated to express in a single expression. To help keep the process transparent, let us divide up the Enjoyment into the following sections:

$$E_{total} \quad = \quad \sum_{1}^{n} E_{single} \; + \; \sum_{1}^{n} E_{nonfinal} \; + \; E_{final} \qquad\qquad \text{Eq. 13.5}$$

In words, the first term to the right of the equals sign sums the total enjoyment of those periods in which you will be single, the second term is the sum of the enjoyment level of all those relationships which do not last, and final term is exactly of the same form as Eq. 13.4, but with "now"

---

[84] Or whatever you choose to call it, happiness, satisfaction, joy ... whatever you've decided is important for you.

replaced by the later time when that final relationship starts, and clearly with E_c replaced by the appropriate value for the final partner.

Now, it is obviously important to stress that it is not appropriate to assume that the enjoyment level E_{min} is appropriate for the short periods of singleness, as the situation of being briefly single and looking is very different from being permanently and decidedly single. Let us define an enjoyment function $E_s(t)$, which, when multiplied by the function $H(t)$ gives the enjoyment level for being single at age t.

For each of the short-term relationships, the enjoyment will again be simply given by an expression of the form of Eq. 13.4, except that the limits on the integral will be t_s and t_e , the times when the relationship started and ended. It is important not to oversimplify here, as the experience at the start of a relationship is different, and so it is not appropriate to assume that 6 2-month relationships with partners of attractiveness level A_z would have the same total enjoyment as one 12-month relationship with one of them.

This far, this is still obvious enough. But when we try to combine this into one neat equation, we face the obstacle that we are dealing with a lot of probabilistic functions (probability of meeting a potential new partner within time t, the probability of deciding to date her (if willing), the probability of deciding to remain with that partner (if willing)), which need to be evaluated in each case before it is possible to even know if there will be further short relationships and periods of singleness or not. This is further complicated by the fact that, even in our very precise definition above at the start of this chapter, it was not clear what would be a person's decision criterion for dating and for remaining with a new partner. For example, if you break up with someone of attractiveness 67, do you then date the next woman of attractiveness 68 or 70 that you meet?[85] Or do you wait for an 80, who might never arrive? The truth is that probably you start out looking for an 80+, but perhaps soon lower your expectations, perhaps even to below the initial level of 67. This will be different for every individual, so it would be deluding ourselves to claim that this can be put in any precise mathematical form.[86]

However, if we make a mathematically limiting but in many cases realistic assumption that the number of relationships that a given individual will have is finite, this allows us to more clearly express the total enjoyment in the form of a series. Let us define the following terms:

---

[85] For reasons of decency and a also in response to a copyright challenge from the estate of Serge Gainsbourg, we have decided not to include this footnote – Ed.

[86] Of course, the true reality in many cases is that even while you're in a relationship, you're always looking out for something better, but we don't approve of that sort of thing. In any case, the mathematics of that are a lot simpler and need not concern us.

Let T_{ri} [87] be the time spent in relationship i ($i=1$ for the first relationship after now)

Let t_{ri} be the age at the beginning of relationship i

Let T_{si} be the time spent single between relationship i and relationship $i+1$

Let t_{si} be the age at the point of ending of relationship i

Let p_i be the probability that relationship i becomes the "final" long-term relationship. (a more morbid but equivalent concept is that you die during it …)

Let $E_i(t)$ be the enjoyment, as a funtion of time, of relationship i, as above.

Let $E_{tot\text{-}ri}$ be the total enjoyment from relationship I (note that this will be in different units from E_i, differing by a first power of time.)

Let $E_{tot\text{-}si}$ be the total enjoyment from the single period between relationship i and relationship $i+1$

We can then define the following totally general expression:

$$
\begin{aligned}
E_{total} \quad = \quad & E_{tot\text{-}s0} \quad + \quad p_1 \int_{tr1}^{\infty} s(t).H(t).E_1\,(t\text{-}t_{r1})dt \\[4pt]
+ \; (1-p_1)\,\{\, & E_{tot\text{-}s1} + \quad E_{tot\text{-}r1} \quad + \quad p_2 \int_{tr2}^{\infty} s(t).H(t).E_2\,(t\text{-}t_{r2})dt \\[4pt]
+ \; (1-p_2)\,\{\, & E_{tot\text{-}s2} + \quad E_{tot\text{-}r2} \quad + \quad p_3 \int_{tr3}^{\infty} s(t).H(t).E_3\,(t\text{-}t_{r3})dt \\[4pt]
+ \; (1-p_3)\,\{\, & E_{tot\text{-}s3} + \quad E_{tot\text{-}r3} \quad + \quad p_4 \int_{tr4}^{\infty} s(t).H(t).E_4\,(t\text{-}t_{r4})dt
\end{aligned}
$$

$$\cdots\cdots$$

$$
+ \; (1-p_i)\,\{\, E_{tot\text{-}ri} \quad + \quad E_{tot\text{-}ri} + \; p_{i+1} \int_{tri+1}^{\infty} s(t).H(t).E_{i+1}\,(t\text{-}t_{ri+1})dt
$$

$$
+ \; \ldots\ldots \qquad \}\}\}\}\ldots\ldots\} \qquad\qquad \text{Eq. 13.6}
$$

It is important to note in the above expression that the brackets indicating multiplication do not close until the end, so that for example the ith term is multiplied by $(1\text{-}p_1)(1\text{-}p_2) \ldots (1\text{-}p_{i\text{-}1})$, i.e. by the probability that

---

[87] Terminology: capital T refers to a duration, small t refers to a point in time or age.

none of the previous *i-1* relationships have been chosen as the final one (if one of them had, then obviously relationship *i* would not happen.[88])

In the above expression, the various E_{tot-ri} and E_{tot-ri} are calculated, in line with the above definition, using the analogues of Eq. 13.4 for finite relationships:

$$E_{tot-ri} \quad = \quad \int_{tri}^{tsi} s(t).H(t).E_i\,(t-t_{ri})dt \qquad \text{Eq. 13.7}$$

and

$$E_{tot-si} \quad = \quad \int_{tsi}^{tri+1} s(t).H(t).E_s\,(t,t-t_{si})dt \qquad \text{Eq. 13.8}$$

where $E_s(age,time)$ is the enjoyment-level of short-term periods as a function of time and of age (i.e. it varies with how old you are and with how long you've been single). In this calculation we have not yet considered the possibility that the person might decide at one point to remain "permanently single", but this possibility can easily be incorporated into the expression by simply modifying the expression for E_s to an appropriate function for this state and then extending the time period (upper limit in equation 13.8) for this single state to infinity.

Clearly there are many over-simplifications in this analysis, yet we believe that even in the absence of precise expressions for each of the functions, it represents a considerable improvement on the simplistic approach outlined in Eqs. 13.1-3. By comparing the total enjoyment values calculated for different options, however complex, you significantly increase the likelihood that you will take the correct decisions – the decisions which are right for you personally. However, it is also clear that only an approach combining the two can ever be truly valid – in the Finite Horizon solution outlined here, we have skipped over the problem of how to use the probability functions defined above to determine the frequency of meeting suitable partners and the attractiveness of these partners, but have just assumed that this calculation has already been done.

The Holy Grail Problem

It is immediately obvious from the analysis of the Finite Horizon problem that the solution to the Holy Grail is easily found by two straightforward steps:

---

[88] Extra-marital relationships and affairs in general will be covered in the sequel – for the purposes of this volume, we assume at least serial monogamy, and periods where this is not the case as considered as single periods.

1. Factor in the implication of time spent calculating, etc. into the enjoyment function of each relationship, *i*, above.
2. Likewise, factor in the implications of this time on the probability of the relationship lasting, in this case perhaps focusing more on the implication that your partner might not be willing to continue.

As a non-mathematical hint, the authors suggest that if you find these terms are dominating the calculation, this book probably is not for you, and maybe you should go back to old-fashioned methods like flipping a coin or deciding if your gut is telling you that you really really want her to have your children.

The best solution is clearly to perform the calculations in your head while making love, thereby not only eliminating time-wastage, but also quite possibly improving the duration of your love-making sessions. However, there is the risk of not being able to make a cold, rational analysis of your current partner's attractiveness at this point, so this particular part of the calculation needs to be done beforehand.

The Stolen Base Problem

It is clear that the approach adopted to solution of the Finite Horizon Problem is also partially effective in addressing the Stolen Base problem. While we will not go through the mathematical details here, it suffices simply to modify this Finite Horizon solution, given above, by inserting the appropriate probability functions for how long it will take to meet suitable partners and the quality of these partners, to then add in a factor indicating how your criteria for deciding what are the requirements for a suitable partner would vary with the length of time you've been single, and finally to extend this process over the full time period that you wish to consider, and not just the period which you have nominally allowed yourself to find a partner. Of course if you have determined, for example, that at age 50, you will just marry the best partner you can find, then clearly the expression from age 50 onwards reduces to a single term, but the approach remains valid.

Approach 2

This approach again begins with the definition and calculation of the function $A_m(x_{1m}, x_{2m}, \ldots, x_{nm})$, as discussed above and in Chapter 11. Let us begin with a very basic analysis in which the function A is considered as a dependent variable in time, *t*. This at least allows us to demonstrate, even to the mathematically illiterate, the principle underlying this approach.

To begin, let us state clearly why this problem is important. It is important because in 97% of cases, men, even non-engineers, only realise that it was a bad idea to break up with their partner *after* the fact, and more specifically, after they've discovered that the only partners they are able to attract anymore are of the ovine variety[89], and therefore somewhat inferior to their previous partners.

It is only at this point that they realise that a careful mathematical analysis of the situation would have demonstrated their diminishing potential and allowed them to avoid this fatal mistake.

The process is simply to calculate values for *A* for each of your past relationships, and to develop an equation for *A*, as a function of time. Let us assume that you are able to achieve this, and that your previous three relationships - for simplicity lets assume the first two relationships each lasted one year, and the most recent one has so far lasted 2 years - have given the following data:

Partner	t	A	
a	0	30	(any port in a storm …)
b	1	60	
c	2	70	

Now, after 2 years with partner *c*, so hence at *t* = 4, you look back at this trend, and you conclude that every year you seem to be able to find a better partner. So surely the same will happen again. However, that would be the road to disillusionment. Because a simple calculation shows that the function *A(t)* is possibly given by

$$A(t) = 30 + 40t - 10t^2$$

So that, substituting in the value for *t* = 4, we'd get

$$A(4) = 30 + 40(4) - 10(16) = 30$$

So that, instead of finding yourself with Naomi Campbell, you're only hope will be to find the twin sister of your first girlfriend, which wasn't exactly what you had in mind.

---

[89] Welsh readers should note that in other countries, and for the purposes of this analysis, this is not considered an improvement, regardless of the quality of wool, due to some inexplicable social stigmas which it is not the purpose nor the right of the authors to question.

How could we have prevented this, and chosen the optimum moment to say "OK, I'll keep what I have"? Obviously, in this very trivial example, we're dealing with a simple differential equation. To maximise A, we need to set

$$dA/dt = 0$$

$$40 - 20t = 0$$

$$t = 2$$

So indeed, a simple analysis that most 12-year-olds can do would have shown you that the partner you met 2 years ago was as good as you could possibly get. She mightn't be exactly what most people would call charming or beautiful or whatever, but she's as good as you're going to get so you just need to accept that!

Of course, the above is all well and good, and theoretically sound, but not very practical, in that it doesn't help you to identify the perfect partner, only the time at which, if you're lucky, you might have found him or her.

The beauty of partial differential analysis is that it allows you to optimse with respect to all the variables simultaneously. So that, with the $n+1$-dimensional space of time plus all the attributes you consider important, you will be able to absolutely maximise the function A, and so not only know when you've found your ideal partner, but also exactly what your ideal partner will be like!

As this chapter is getting far to long, we leave the challenge of finding this ideal partner in the real, 3-dimensional world as an exercise for the reader.

Approach 3

For those who prefer a simple and less mathematical analysis, the following approach, while significantly less elegant than the previous two, has been found effect for male engineers in 99% of cases:

The approach involves three stages:

1. Ask yourself the following questions:
   - am I an engineer?
   - is my partner a human being of the appropriate sex? (i.e. the one you like)
   - does s/he consent to sleep with me occasionally?
   - has s/he been convicted of mass-murder and/or killed ≥ 2 ex-husbands/ wives?

2. Answer the questions:

3. Tabulate your answers. If you answered yes to three of the questions, and no to at most one, then chances are pretty good that you've maxed out, it's hard to imagine you will do any better, indeed one wonders how you've done so well.

If additionally, your one "no" refers to the fourth question, then this technique's accuracy increases from just 99% to 99.9% - although this difference is less significant when the requirement is added that the engineer in question be alive and able to answer the questions in the statistical survey.

Approach 4

So how do you know if you've yet reached your peak of attractiveness, or if there's even better to come? If you're at the stage of being able to match your shoes and socks, does that mean that someday soon you'll be able to match your shirts with your pants, or does it mean that your feet will soon smell so bad that you'll need a nose-clip to change your socks?

Luckily, both Leibniz and Newton, the two men who independently invented calculus, suffered from odoriferous feet, and indeed Newton never married[90] because by the time he realised this, it was too late. This is thought to be what finally induced him to invent differential calculus. In Leibniz's case, it was due to a similar experience but of the opposite kind, where he married young only to realise that had he waited until he was a famous philosopher, he could have slept with numerous college sophomores.

Therefore, in simple terms, the calculus was designed to help engineers and scientists understand where they are on what we may term their "life-curve"[91]. While of course there may be many life curves, each emphasising a different quality, trait or odour, in this analysis we focus exclusively on the area of attractiveness.

---

[90] What's the fixation with Newton's sex life, or lack of it? This is about the third time that's come up. Can't they find anyone more interesting to discuss? What kind of psychological issues does it reveal .. that haven't already been revealed? – [Editor]

[91] Since the time of Newton and Leibniz, several further uses for calculus have been discovered, but it is still considered too unimportant to be taught in most US high schools – indeed this is why prospective Engineering candidates are urged to take a calculus course in their Freshman year, as they are probably the only college students who might already be on the downward part of their curve.

Furthermore, for completeness, it's important to realise that this refers to attractiveness to "average" women – of course, as women differ, so will their valuations of the different traits of men and of male engineers. But recall that this analysis is being done without one specific woman in mind, but rather as a general measure of "appropriate expectations", and as such, it's appropriate to consider only the average. That said, an engineer who, for example, is exclusively interested in red-heads, might want to take the average of red-heads rather than of the whole female population, to get the most accurate answer – this difference is unlikely to be relevant unless that particular subset has a particular preference which differs markedly from the norm, for example, if it were known that red-heads preferred balding men[92] while brunettes preferred men with full heads of hair.[93]

So, what both Leibniz and Newton had in mind was a way to measure the rates at which our various traits are changing, and even the rates at which the rates of change are changing, and so on. With this knowledge and an appropriate algorithm relating our traits to our attractiveness, it then becomes trivial to work out where we stand on our life-curve, and so to decide whether or not we should formalise our relationship with our current partner, leave things as they stand, or start actively looking for an upgrade.

As this book is targeted at engineers, we're going to assume that we don't need to explain calculus or it's notation. If there are any Humanities or Business majors reading this, the best way to think about calculus is that it's a form of magic, exactly like the magic you see every day in your job when you put cut up potatoes into hot oil and they come out as fries. You don't need to understand how it works to benefit from it.

Let us then consider a simplified model in which an engineer calculates that the most important attributes which affect his attractiveness to women are:

---

[92] Unfortunately there is no firm evidence to support this, although an optimistic proof has been sketched by a balding redhaired professor of mathermatics at the university of Illinois along the lines of evolutionary selection and making choices that maximize the possibility that the offspring will get a chance to reproduce. It's a fact that the sons of red-headed parents are more likely to be themselves red-headed, and it is well known that, while for most men, balding significantly reduces their attractiveness to women, in the case of red-heads, it makes very little difference. It's not clear if this is due to the fact that their overall attractiveness was already so low or because of the specific negative effect of red hair. And of course, while it's also known that red-headed women are typically considered very attractive, they are of course unlikely to go bald. So, in theory, a red-headed woman would have less to lose on an evolutionary level by dating a balding guy than would a blonde or a brunette.

[93] .. and typically, there is evidence to support this one ... again, please don't shoot the messenger – and if you must, it was the guy in the bookstore who sold you this, not the authors.

- his appearance
- his income
- his wit and charm
- his bowling average
- his ability to calculate things

Now, it's important already at this stage to highlight a potential drawback with this approach, for which the authors cannot be held legally responsible (we've checked). There is no guarantee that the engineer's evaluation of what is important, and the relative weight he gives to it, is an accurate reflection of what an average woman might feel. For example, in the case of this specific engineer, we asked him to weight each of the attributes proportionally to it's relative importance, to get a total of 100. We then asked a random selection of non-engineering women to do the same exercise.[94] Let's look at the results:

	Engineer's weighting	Women's weighting
Appearance	23.61	50
Income	24.07	35
Wit & Charm	11.36	15
Bowling Average	14.60	0
Ability to Calculate Things	26.36	0

It's clear that there are some minor discrepancies which could lead the engineer to reach a false conclusion even with precise calculations, if he were not to first validate his assumptions with a statistically significant number of women – an unlikely eventuality, since if he knew a statistically significant number of women, he wouldn't be buying this book. We should also point out here that we're perfectly aware that the use of the term "statistically significant" in this context is totally without meaning, or at best highly imprecise, but we can't be perfect all the time.

Now, in reality, the variation of each of the above factors with time will be a still quite complex phenomenon, involving positive delta-functions for salary increases and negative delta functions for purchases of brown shoes. But with a little smoothing, for example calculating the averages

---

[94] Political correctness prevents us from recounting in detail the level of difficulty we had explaining the concepts of weighting and numbers adding up to 100 to non-engineers. Let's just say that we ended up doing the exercise with different coloured jelly-beans and that the researcher who led the work is still in therapy, as are at least two of the interviewees. There's probably a lesson there somewhere.

over each year rather than on a complete time continuum, it should be possible to get a relatively accurate estimate. Let us imagine that the situation with this particular engineer is as follows:

- He's in a good paying job, let's say at age 30 he's earning $80,000/year and this is increasing at a rate of $5,000/year, and he expects it to continue to increase at about this rate indefinitely[95]. So this is clearly one aspect of his life that is improving, with a precise rate of $dI/dt = 5$ (in the following, and in the weighting, we're assuming that the units have already been defined, in this case income is measured in units of $1000/year).

$$dI/dt \ = \ 5$$

- He's getting older, so each year losing some hair, getting wrinkles, gaining weight, and so on, so his physical appearance (*PA*) is decreasing. Let us arbitrarily define his appearance on a 0-100 scale to be 50 (yes, we know it's unrealistically high, but it makes no difference to the analysis), and let's say that it's decreasing at a rate of 3 / year. Therefore $PA = 50 - 3t$, where t is measured from the time when $PA = 50$.
- But there's also the fact that his dress style is changing. Let's consider this his Dress appearance (*DA*). On the one hand, he now has more money to buy clothes, on the other hand his taste is getting increasingly outdated, his laundry habits are getting worse, the yellow stains under his armpits have expanded and people have given up trying to help him with occasional words of advice. This can really only be approximated by a quadratic equation in which in his younger years the purchasing power (linear) term dominates, but as he gets older, the quadratic term induces a rapid decline. Clearly the linear term is related both to age (more clothes) and income, *I*, (better clothes). So we get, for example, $DA = 5t + 0.5\,I - 0.125\,t^2$, where we've used the letter t to denote age to create further confusion.
- Combining these two, we get total appearance, $A = DA + PA = k + 2t + 0.5I - 0.125\,t^2$. The constant, k, which we could fix to get the current value = 50 doesn't really interest us, what we want to know is how this factor is changing over time, dA/dt. And it's clear that this is given by:

$$dA/dt \ = \ 2 + 0.5\,dI/dt - 0.25\,t$$

---

[95] We chose to leave him with this one illusion …

From above, $dI/dt = 5$, which means that $dA/dt = 4.5 - 0.25\ t$ .. suggesting that the engineer's total appearance will improve until the age of 18 – pretty much until he enters engineering school, then start to go downhill, at first slowly, but getting increasingly fast as the quadratic term takes over. As he's 30 now, this should give him some pause for thought.

- Now, even an engineer himself will realise that time spent in the company of other engineers doing engineering does not make a person more witty and charming. While even in college some remnants of pre-engineering wit may have remained, it's safe to say that these will be dwindling rapidly to the point where a prospective partner would probably be ashamed to introduce him to any of her friends, or even to their pets. Let us represent this decline mathematically as

$$dW/dt = -2$$

- To minimise further distractions from this already mind-numbing example, we're going to assume that until the onset of senility the engineer's ability to calculate things will remain pretty much constant, while his bowling average will not change since he doesn't actually bowl. It was interesting that as a non-bowler he should have chosen this as a trait which would be important to women, but we're mathematicians, not psychologists. So:

$$dB/dt = 0 \quad ;$$

$$dC/dt = 0$$

- This then leaves us with the total rate of change of attractiveness, AT, appropriately weighted, as:

$$dAT/dt = 23.61\ dA/dt + 24.07\ dI/dt + 11.36\ dW/dt$$
$$+ 0 + 0$$

$$= (23.61)\ (4.5 - 0.25\ t) + 24.07\ (5) + 11.36\ (-2)$$

$$= 203.875 - 5.905\ t$$

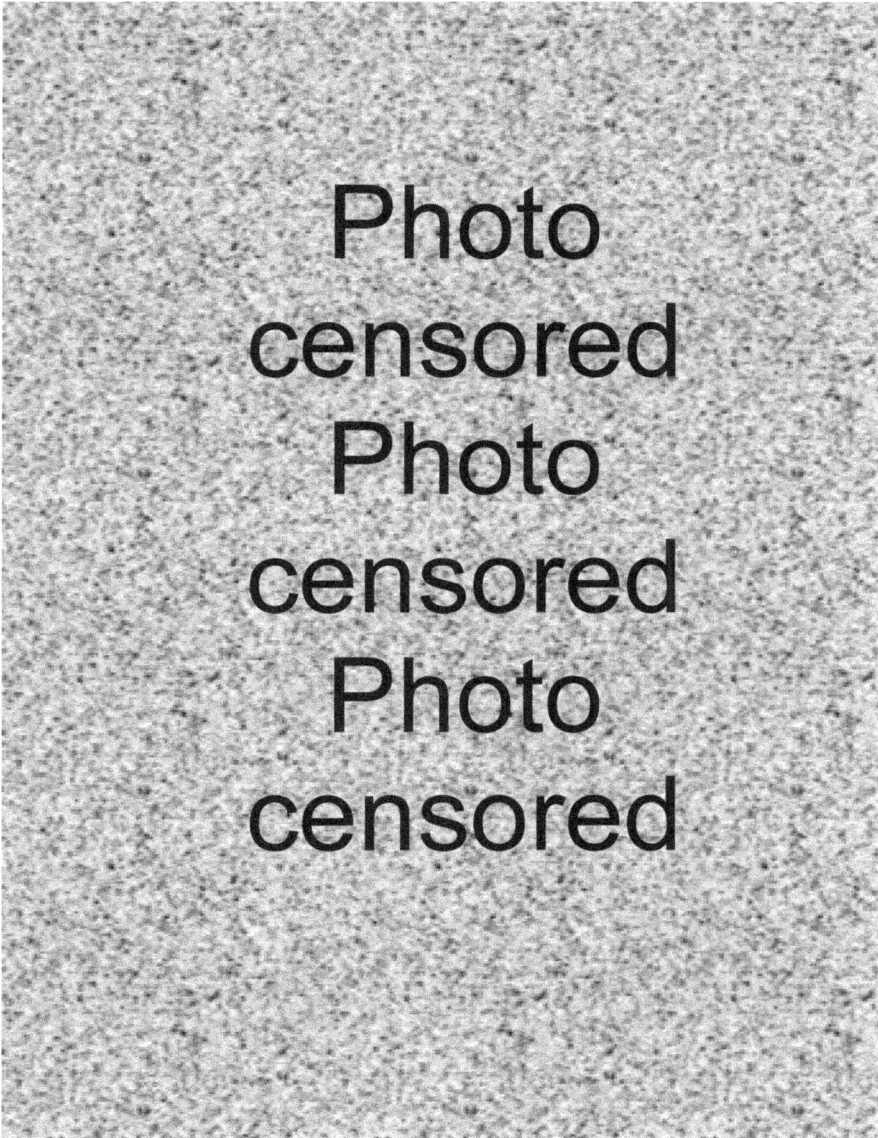

Figure 16.3 "A typical Engineer" – From a selection of over 50 photos, this one photo was judged by 31% of women to best represent the aesthetic qualities they associated with Engineers. Coincidentally, this is actually a photo of an Engineer, ~~XXXXXXX XXXXXXX~~ (name censored due to legal action – Ed), who graduated from the University of Wisconsin Electronic Engineering Dept in 1994. He is known to be somewhat sensitive about people seeing this photo.

Setting the derivative equal to zero, we calculate that the age of peak attractiveness for this particular engineer, by his own calculations, is 34½ years. This can be seen graphically in the chart of his life-curve, shown below. In this simple example, obviously inspection alone could have generated the information, however in a real life situation with many factors to be considered, using the techniques of calculus simplifies matters considerably, and provides the further advantage of highlighting which terms are most critical in driving the decline, offering the remote but tantalising possibility that it might be possible to work on some of these.

So if this 30-year-old engineer is now in a steady relationship, however unlikely that may be, he needs to be aware that over the next 4½ years, his attractiveness will continue to increase ... maybe he could do better?? But after that, he needs to think very carefully about discarding a willing partner, as his rapidly declining attractiveness will make it increasing difficult for him to find another.

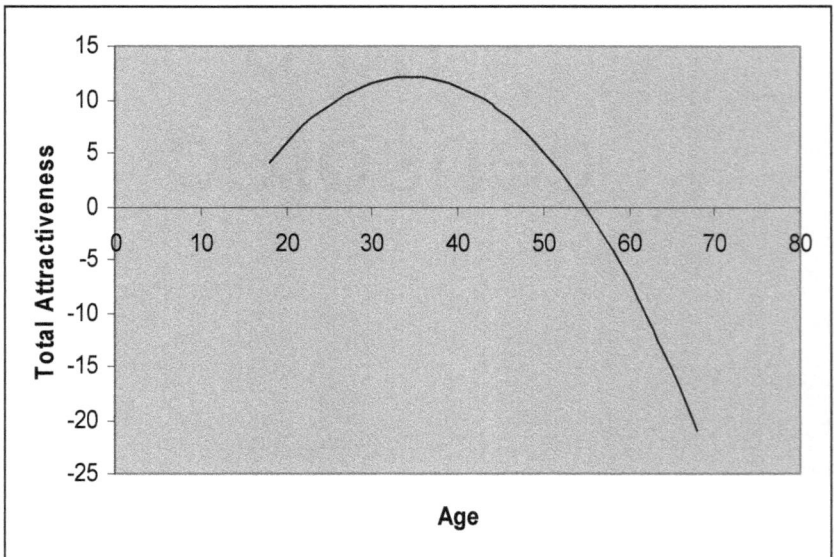

Fig 16.4 The Engineer's attractiveness starts off low, and increases very slightly before diving into the negative range of utter repulsiveness. As the analysis indicates, woe betide the engineer who doesn't realize that he's past his peak and who gives up the chance of a relationship with a potentially willing partner under the delusion that he can do better!

Hopefully this long and tedious chapter will have taught you something about how to evaluate your current situation and compare it to possible alternatives. You don't actually have to work through all the math to capture that thought process involved, and like much of the material in this book, while the presentation may be somewhat ironic in style, the concepts involved have a certain undeniable logical validity about them, which would have come through clearly if the writing had been more coherent.

But enough of the carefree banter, we now move on to the serious question of marriage:

Chapter 17   Marriage – Is It Necessarily the End of Happiness?

Pretty much.

Chapter 17a   Marriage, Is It Necessarily the End of Happiness? (Revised[96])

So you've finally done it. You have faithfully employed all of the lessons described in the previous chapters. You have diligently followed all of the complicated proofs and postulates. You have made yourself a better man. And yes, yes…finally….you have found a woman. And you have dated, and perhaps even had sex (with her). And you have fallen in love or a reasonable facsimile, as explained in Chapter 16, and now you are married.

And of course the stupid thing is that you didn't read to the end of the book before you got married, thinking that getting the woman was the end of it. And now, as the honeymoon period ends, and your new wife stops working out, stops applying make-up, stops shaving her legs, starts wearing sweatpants more often and is no longer shy about flatulence, you start to wonder….

Is marriage the end of happiness?

This has been a question asked by many distinguished engineers and scientists throughout history[97], the connection being that unhappiness generally leads to the best engineering science[98]. However, even if you

---

[96] Following very wise advice from one of our early reviewers. She denies that her opinion was related to her being married to one of the authors …

[97] McCabe and Thiele, "*Escaping the Wife through Distillation Technology,*" or Bernoulli, "*Mia moglie e' pazza!*" [NB Not to be confused with his other marital classics "*Mia moglie puzza!*" or "*Sessanta-nove con mia moglie? Preferisco mangiare la pizza*"].

[98] Hence Germany's leading position in most engineering fields.

are not a distinguished engineer, you can also share the unhappiness of marriage.

[Note: On the advice of our legal counsel, we would kindly ask that all the engineers who are reading this chapter who in fact ARE married and happy about it, please skip to the next section. We would feel badly if we were to bring any of such individuals out of their ignorant state of bliss with concrete arguments as to why they should feel unhappy. Not only would we feel badly, we might also liable for psychiatric damages and so on.]

When things go badly, our natural engineering instinct is to turn to failure mode analysis (typically known as FMEA, Failure Mode and Effects Analysis) as a tool for understanding. For example, when a bridge collapses or an airplane crashes, investigators are on the spot immediately to figure out what went wrong and to correct the mistakes for the future. It is through this systematic process that we as a society make progress, especially in safety. The interesting observation, though, is that although we have become better at avoiding tragedies like airplane crashes, the unhappiness of the average engineer in the average marriage has not decreased significantly in the last several decades[99].

Using the FMEA methodology, it is first important to understand the process inputs, hence we start with a very basic process flow diagram, shown in Figure 17.1.

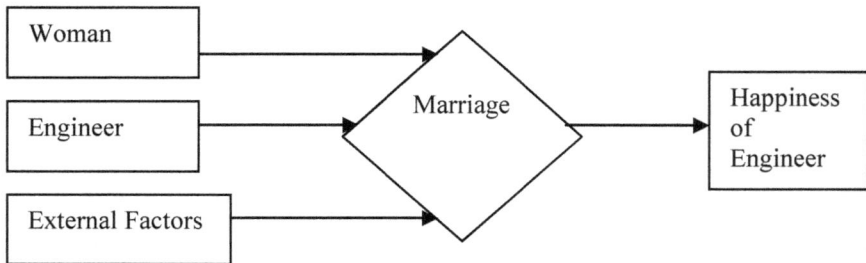

Figure 17.1 Simplified overview of FEMA analysis of Engineer's marriage.

One could argue that Marriage is a state rather than a process, however in such a case it would be path independent, therefore rendering some

---

[99] It would have been interesting to get marriage statistics over the past several decades to demonstrate this, but we haven't bothered – we don't think this assertion is likely to be challenged.

aspects of this book rather meaningless. By defining marriage as a process, we can apply all of the characterization tools painstakingly developed for other relatively unimportant areas such as energy production, transportation, and agriculture.

With a process viewpoint, we also need to define an output. There are many potential outputs of marriage, including children, suburban homes, alimony payments and homicide, however we focus on the key output that concerns us here: the happiness of the engineer. In fact, this output is so important that we designate it the "critical Y" or critical output. Clearly other outputs will occur, and may very well have an influence on the happiness output, but we ignore feedback effects for the moment.

The inputs to the process are grouped for simplicity in three major clusters, the wife, the engineer and so called "external factors". Each of these inputs clusters, or X's have characteristics which influence the process and critical Y. In the FMEA methodology, we analyze each of these input clusters and understand how they can go wrong. The root causes are then evaluated for their effects and severity and detectability. Clearly, more severe effects are of more concern, but so are those which are difficult to detect. Even though the fact that your wife is becoming rapidly obese may be regrettable, it is easily detectable, allowing the engineer to take corrective action (e.g. suggest joining a health club, introducing flesh eating parasites into her breakfast cereal etc.). With that framework we charge ahead into the process input analysis.

Input Cluster 1: Wife

This is the most obvious place to start, as it is quite easy to recognize the defects. Some of the most common failure modes include: weight gain[100], poor hygiene, inattention to personal appearance, and development of annoying personal habits. In addition to these factors, which are directly related to the wife, there is the general category of nagging, which is a defective behaviour mode which is programmed to initiate approximately 24 hours after the honeymoon concludes. These are the failure modes that most engineers, indeed men in general, complain about. Clearly, this

---

[100] It is little known that in addition to the universal law of gravitation, Sir Isaac Newton also proposed the less well known post-marital law mass increase:

$$W = W_0 exp(C_1 t)$$

where

W = mass of wife at time t

t = time in years

$C1$ = weight gain constant, a strong function of exercise and fried cheese curd consumption

cluster of failure modes is something to worry about, since their effect (loss of attractiveness), severity (can make engineer somewhat unhappy) and frequency (they occur with devastating frequency across all countries) are quite high. The causes are quite clear, that is the wife is generally "letting herself go" after the long quest for a suitable mate. The cause of the nagging phenomena has yet to be understood, but is likely deeply ingrained in the emotional makeup of all women.

As another part of the FMEA, it is important to identify existing controls which may prevent the failure mode. Unfortunately, most men, directly after marriage, are too much in a state of shock to systematically implement a control system for their new wife. After a few attempts at humor (hey honey, boy your legs are getting hairier than mine ! hah hah) followed by violent response, the average engineer gives up on controls. There are, however, improvement steps which can be taken to remedy practically all of these failure modes. These steps will be outlined in our expensive new book "Marriage for Engineers."

Input Cluster 2: The Engineer

Although it sounds like blaming the victim, it is all too true that the engineer can be at fault for his own unhappiness. Aside from errors in judgment regarding wife selection or entering the marriage process altogether, there are other failure modes which often occur.

- Unclear Expectations: When the average desperate engineer thinks about marriage, he thinks only about the really positive aspects of marriage. For example, not having to do things alone, someone who can cook more than a can of beans, and a constant supply of free sex. He never considers that these things are also present in most federal prisons.
- Insufficient inspection: With most major acquisitions, there is generally a disclosure of some sort, usually written in exotic legal language, explaining what kind of disasters could happen if you go through with the deal. For example, when you buy a house, the disclosure may tell about the every-once-in-a-while moisture in the basement that leads to mutant mold spores that will kill you and everyone you know, and everyone you don't know too. Even though most of us skip over these things, at least they are there. Also, there are warranties associated with most major deals, like money-back guarantees or free repairs and so on. Unfortunately, with marriage, there are generally no disclosures and no

warranties. This is of course known to you at some intellectual level when you are dating, but the reality doesn't hit until later.

- Speculation: This is a very common failure mode, especially when some difficulties are encountered in the marriage. The engineer starts to reassess previous options, playing out scenarios from his past. Usually this involves previous relationships or wild speculation about women met during chance encounters (e.g. at the grocery store... "I know from the way that chick asked me which aisle the salad dressing was in that she wanted me..")

Cluster 3: External Factors

- Other Women, the Increased attractiveness principle: Referring back to the multiple dating chapter – a carryover principle is that your attractiveness will increase 10-fold after you are married (mathematical proof is in progress). By marrying, you have eliminated several of the most common defects identified by women, the inability to commit to a relationship, being unattractive to other women, and so on. The trap is that if you leave your wife for this other woman, then you will need to commit to her, which leads you into the same thing again. So to avoid lots of alimony payments, lawyers fees, and potentially deadly gunfire, it is best to stick with whomever you have.
- Single Friends: When you were single, you probably had friends who became married before you. At first it was like old times, you would see them fairly often and go out with them. But gradually, the contacts broke off and the guys disappeared from the face of the earth. The reason this happens is not so much that the married guys become busy or have other priorities, the fact of the matter is that they simply do not want to see their single buddies anymore. There is probably nothing worse for the newly married guy than to see his single friends go off and do really exciting things (they weren't of course exciting before) such as try to unsuccessfully pick up girls at the engineering library, while he has to go home to the Mrs. It is a complex mixture of envy and regret which ultimately impacts the critical Y.

Using a simple scaling method, such as factoring severity, occurrence and detectability, one can generate a Pareto chart showing the top failure modes contributing to sub-optimal happiness. Given limited resources, it is important to focus on the top contributors and develop action plans around them. For example, if your wife getting fat is the root cause of your relative unhappiness, you can brainstorm various ideas to improve the situation. You could do things such as buying her a membership at a health club, buying low fat foods or moving to a famine-devastated country.

For legal and ethical reasons, improvement measures are outside the scope of this book, left at least temporarily to the imagination of the reader. Even at this level, the FMEA analysis can at least bring a level of understanding to why your critical Y, your happiness, is not currently optimized. By segmenting the root causes to a detailed level, we at least know why we are miserable.

But the main question remains, *is marriage the end of happiness?*

We did a detailed analysis of all the practical positives associated with marriage. These boiled down to two. The first of these, more regular sex, was found, upon closer analysis, to be illusory and not supported by any data – apparently the investigators who proposed this theory assumed that "sleeping with" was necessarily the euphemism for sex, whereas among many married couples it was actually no more than a precise description of their sleeping arrangements, where the primary objective was to ensure that the partner wasn't having sex with anyone else.

The second benefit, perhaps more tangible, was an end to expensive dates. In the chapter on Market Research, the example of the appeal of an expensive sports car was mentioned, and the analogy to peacock feathers. The appeal in each case was not so much anything tangible as the demonstration that one was so "well off" that one could spend excess money/energy on something as impractical as a sports car or an exotic tail. Analogously, when you invite a woman on a date, she is likely to be very impressed by the "sunk cost" of your date – the amount of your investment in the date which is absolutely non-refundable. So you're under pressure to spend a lot of money. It may even be less important to her that she enjoys it – most women would be more seduced by a $500 meal which they found bland than by a very tasty $5 meal. It's all part of those evolutionary preferences for a partner who will be a good long-term provider.

Marriage however, puts an end to this. Because suddenly the resources you would be investing are not only yours, but also your wife's. And suddenly the $5 meal is much less of a problem. So far, this sounds great. However, only until you realize that the $495 that you've saved isn't yours to keep, no, it'll go towards new curtains for the living room, and guess who will be expected to fit and install these?[101]

Figure 17.2 A photo of a happily married couple, disproving the myth that marriage is necessarily the end of happiness.

So, Is marriage necessarily the end of happiness?

The above evidence and logic appears pretty damning. However, as indicated above (between the lines perhaps), once you are married, it's probably easier to stay married to the same person than to deal with all the hassle and alimony payments involved in a messy divorce. So, without in any way wanting to cheat our readers of an honest and balanced perspective, we have to deal with the unfortunate reality that one of us is married, and that his wife will one day read this, and therefore it would be

---

[101] And even worse, be expected to have an opinion as to what pattern and colour they should be …

very preferable for the answer to the question to be along the lines of "No".

Within this context, we consider the notion of a Paradigm shift. Most of us recognize a paradigm shift as a largely meaningless recommendation you get from overpaid management consultants when your business is almost totally fucked, but not quite fucked enough that you can't afford to pay overpaid management consultants to complete the job.

What is the paradigm shift of marriage? The key is not to judge marriage by the same criteria you would use to judge your single life. As you get married, you are basically exchanging variety, lust and freewheeling sex[102] for contentedness. How good of an exchange is this? Well, remarkably enough, there is a relatively scientific answer to this:

Essentially, making this trade is akin to trading in a dopamine high for a serotonin high.[103]

As with so many scientific answers, this isn't particularly clear, so let us explain in a bit more detail:

The human brain has evolved to "reward" us for doing things that are evolutionarily favourable (like sex) by releasing chemicals in certain parts of our brain which give us feelings of pleasure. We're all familiar with a runner's high being due to endorphins, for example, and it's also well known that opiates are closely associated with "pure pleasure" such as we enjoy when we eat really good food. However, there are also other types of activities and states which are "pleasurable", and marriage can in many cases be viewed as a transition from one of these to the other.

Researchers have learned that the brain rewards the striving, competitive aspects of life – which for our engineer would involve things like the challenge of meeting new women – with the neurotransmitter dopamine. We enjoy the challenge and we enjoy "winning" because of dopamine.

But there's a rub: the prize itself doesn't bring a dopamine high. As far as dopamine is concerned, even marrying the most wonderful woman in the universe is a downer, because you've necessarily lost the right and the need to "compete", and it's the competing that gives us the dopamine high. To the dopamine addict, the idea of a perfect marriage is like the idea of the average golf pro who one day wins the British Open, and then is told that the only downside is that he's not allowed to play golf anymore. Would he make that trade? Men spend years of their life "competing" for women, then once they've finally got good at it and

---

[102] Also, be honest with yourself about how much sex you were really getting when you were single. Remember, you're an engineer, so you're likely one of the few who's having more sex after marriage than before.

[103] Daniel Nettle, Royal Institution, London, and other workers. Best reference is the book "*Happiness*" by Daniel Nettle (Oxford University Press). [and this is a real reference!!]

started to enjoy it, they meet their wife and suddenly they can't play anymore. Ouch!

However, it's not all bad news. The brain had to evolve a compensatory mechanism to allow us to enjoy the fruits of our competition and so to have some form of stability. As a single person, you may have a lot of excitement, but not so much contentment, since the two are somewhat mutually exclusive – it's hard to be both totally content and still be driven to change from your current content state! When you're in a state of contentment and feeling really satisfied, what you're likely experiencing is a serotonin high – actually more a relaxed feeling of wellbeing than the euphoric high that comes from dopamine. As an engineer, you've probably experienced this kind of thing *after* exams in school and college.

For the golf pro, he knows that he's won the British Open, and that nobody can ever take that away from him.

One way, therefore, to look at marriage is not so much as the end of happiness *per se*, but rather as a transition to a different type of happiness, where comparing the two is like comparing apples and oranges. Basically, you need to ask yourself are you ready to accept fewer euphoric dopamine highs in return for a more regular serotonin high?[104]

With this in mind, we've reached the political conclusion that marriage is not necessarily the end of happiness per se, but *caveat emptor*, be aware of what you're getting into!

---

[104] there are so many caveats to this analysis, including for example the assumption that marriage will make you more content (with about a 50% divorce rate this is dubious). We suspect that even non-engineers reading this analysis will see the flaws in the reasoning, but as mentioned in the introduction, we "prefer" not to.

Chapter 18   Conclusions

Well, this has been a pleasant jaunt through the rarely associated worlds of mathematics, dating and macromolecular hydrodynamics. We've certainly emerged from the journey wiser and more satisfied than when we set out.

But we're engineers, so we can't be satisfied with intangible benefits like wisdom and happiness – instead we want to know, in concrete terms, what has this book taught us, and does it justify our investment of $16.99 (estimated at time of writing).

Fortunately, on this occasion, the answer is a resounding "yes" – and one can conclude with reasonable certainty that this book probably represents the pinnacle of your investments in this life – one of those rare decisions you'll look back on with your grandchildren and recall with great nostalgia. Of course, by then the book will be recognized as a classic, your grandchildren will already have their own well-worn e-versions, and perhaps some kindly great-uncle may have left them his personal paper copy in his will, with the advice that they carefully peruse its contents before making any important life-altering decisions. So it will not be easy for your grandchildren to understand the great prescience which you displayed to bravely invest your $19.99 at a time when doing so was considered neither profitable nor popular ... but since you're their grandfather, they'll probably humour you anyway.

But for now, let us focus on the more immediate benefits that you are already seeing in your life today, which, let us recall, are only a pale shadow of those which will accrue to you over the next few years as you put the concepts of this book into practice. [You may also want to tear out these conclusions and use them as a "cheat-sheet" to refresh your memory whenever you're faced with an unexpected potential dating situation].

The core of the book was divided into 4 main sections. In the first section, we examined the phenomenon of being an engineer from the perspective of the world of dating. It was painful, but we forced ourselves to be honest and realistic. As the saying goes, recognizing the problem is half the solution. Unfortunately in our case, it turned out to be the wrong half, as our research showed that no amount of self-examination or soul-searching alone would alone make a tangible difference in the dating lives of engineers.

But, far from being discouraged, we intrepidly passed to the second section, in which we provided some basic tools. While of limited mathematical sophistication, these strategies and knowledge, properly applied, can bring the average engineer's performance in dating situations all the way up from appalling to as high as mediocre – although we cannot promise mediocrity in all cases.

This section began with an explanation of the probability model of dating, and then went on to show how – statistically – you should be having more sex than you are. Which begs the obvious question of why this is the case. So we explained a couple of key concepts which are central to understanding the reasons why, in general, engineers don't get laid as much as they might like.

But here is where this book differs from our many imitators. Others would produce a dramatic conclusion, a complex proof, a scientific explanation, and then rest on their laurels. Yes, the reader would feel wiser for the knowledge, he may even feel reassured that he's not alone … but he's not significantly nearer to getting laid than he was before he started.[105] Instead, we provided practical tools to help address this issue, for example the clear, simple algorithm which enables you to ask someone out on a date without requiring any interpersonal skills or social understanding – we've programmed it all for you – you just follow the steps and you can't go wrong.[106]

At this early stage, we refrained from discussing the mathematical practicalities of sex itself, secure in the assumption that very few readers will achieve the level of suaveness likely to lead to sex before they have time to read the relevant chapters in the third section.

---

[105] Yes, we checked. Out of 38 women interviewed, not one was remotely more likely to sleep with a man just because he could give a scientific explanation for why he wasn't getting enough sex. Let's be realistic, if this were not the case, do you think we'd be spending our time writing books??

[106] To be clear, this doesn't mean that the person will agree to go out with you – just that the reason for the refusal will not be due to flaws in the way you asked.

The third section brought our analysis to the next level. The basic premise of the book was that we engineers can and should use our superior logical and mathematical reasoning ability to be more successful at dating. This section showed you how. Applying techniques well beyond the intellectual range of lawyers or marketers, we showed how to

- Use linear algebra to identify your ideal date from a group,
- Apply game theoretical solutions to competitive situations where you must compete with others to capture your ideal date's heart.
- Apply the theory of atomic orbitals to the problem of dating multiple partners without losing the one(s) you most care about.

And finally, now that you'd reached the stage where sex was becoming a realistic possibility, we provided a full description of the two alternative analyses of the process. Undoubtedly those of you who have studied these will have found that the whole experience of intercourse will have become more satisfying for both you and your partner.[107]

In the fourth section we looked at really advanced topics, which become relevant once you've entered into a relationship. Firstly is the eternal question of whether to remain in the current relationship or to break-up and hope to find someone better. Beginning from first principles, we derived an exact equation which allows you to make this decision for yourself in the knowledge that you've maximised your happiness expectation value.

However, given that one possible outcome of this calculation – namely, staying with one's partner forever – could potentially lead to marriage, we then provided an engineering analysis of marriage to decide scientifically if it really represents the end of happiness. In order to make this chapter a little bit longer, in our first revision of the book we adapted the title to include the word "necessarily", thereby avoiding stating the obvious.

The first appendix contains a very advanced topic, which we recognize even many engineers may not find easy to follow. Now that your personal relationship had been sorted out, you were probably asking what you could do to help others. This appendix focuses on the most important element of that, namely how to help your engineering colleagues meet more prospective partners, while at the same time avoiding any situation in which it wouldn't be possible to separate them if the need arose. The theoretical concepts involved have been analysed by Chemical Engineers for decades, but their application to mixing engineers rather than molecules has only recently received the attention it deserved.

---

[107] To some extent this conclusion rests on your having started out with somewhat suboptimal technique. Some readers have also questioned the use of the word "satisfying" in a context which differs from that in general use.

If you've completed the whole book and applied the techniques for some time, it's unlikely that you'll have found time in your hectic social life to be reading these conclusions. If you're still reading, that may indicate that this volume alone hasn't been sufficient to overcome your particularly dire personal and social issues – and we encourage you to purchase Volume II of this series, which should be on the shelves of good bookstores everywhere in the Fall.[108]

A Philosophical Digression.

Rather than end this fine intellectual project with a cheap plug for the sequel, it seemed more appropriate, and more high-brow, to conclude with another irrelevant venture into the world of great philosophers. And to conclude with one of the great unanswered questions: Who among the great philosophers can claim[109] the title of "The Engineers' Philosopher"?

Our investigation into this yielded a very surprising answer.

If you asked most engineers which philosopher they most identify with, many would cite Leibniz, who co-invented the Calculus, Descartes who gave 2/3 of his name to Cartesian geometry[110], or Bertrand Russell who put so much work into the Principia Mathematica.

However, our historical analysis suggests that it is Spinoza to whom Engineers should turn when looking for their philosophical role-model. Even a quick perusal of Spinoza's biography[111] produces compelling evidence, and several details that suggest he might have had the same issues with dating that afflict so many engineers.

- At the age of 23, typical age of the newly-graduated Engineer, Spinoza was captivated by the daughter of his teacher, van den Enden. She, however, oblivious to his clear intellectual brilliance, rejected him for a richer pupil. How similar to the many engineers who are rejected in college either for rich frat-boys with expensive cars or for those studying something likely to make them rich, even if not wise (for example law or commerce)?
- One of his Spinoza's contemporary biographers, JM Lucas, who knew him will, says that while he "did not condemn marriage for

---

[108] Exact year hasn't been specified at time of publication.

[109] *Can* claim, but assuredly would choose not to ..

[110] the other third apparently came from the Australian swimmer Ian Thorpe, although there are some time and causality issues with this idea.

[111] Roger Scruton, Oxford University Press, 1986

others, he rejected it for himself," perhaps fearing the ill-temper of a woman, or perhaps finding the idea incompatible with his scholarly interests. Again similar to engineers in so many ways.

- o On the one hand, there is the clear analytical approach, endorsed fully by this book, which suggests fully understanding the risks of marriage before entering into it.
- o On the other hand, though, is the flawed logic[112] which allows him to use his scholarly pursuits as a reason to avoid a relationship, so missing the key point that all the scholarly pursuits in the world are worthless if they don't help you get laid at some point.[113]

- However, the aspect of Spinoza's life which most closely resonates with the experiences of engineers is that of rejection. Engineers who have tried dating know all about rejection, and Spinoza got some rejections which put even many engineers' rejections to shame. An example, which coincides almost word for word with the rejection one of the authors received as an undergraduate[114], is the rejection Spinoza received from all the Jewish women[115] in his community in Amsterdam. Some of the key elements of this rejection were:

> *"cursed be you by day and cursed be you by night; cursed be you when you lieth down, and cursed be you when you riseth up; cursed be you when you goeth out, and cursed be you when you cometh in .... The Lord will be kindled against you and bring down upon you all the curses which are wrtten in the book of the law; ..... nobody may communicate with you, nor show you any favour, nor be within four cubits of you ..."*

(... it goes on, but I think it's already becoming clear to our readers that even the cleverest philosopher would have difficulty interpreting this as an invitation for an intimate date the following Tuesday evening.)

How many engineers do not hear these or similar words every weekend when they try out their charm on prospective dates in social settings? So let us go forth confident in the knowledge that we too, like Spinoza, have the potential to overcome even the most discouraging starts, and that even if we never get laid, we can at least, as Spinoza did, leave behind a

---

[112] See the "Laska phenomenon" referenced in the analysis of Q6 of the self-evaluation quiz.

[113] At least according to Dr. Freud, and who are we do disagree?

[114] Before becoming the expert in the mathematical dating techniques outlined in this book, of course.

[115] And men, but that's not the point here ...

metaphysical theory that will not be shown to be seriously flawed by a German guy until long after we're dead[116].

And if that doesn't motivate you, then we don't know what will ...

---

[116] Or, given that we're engineers, maybe just build some bridges that will fall after we're dead, or reactors that will explode, or silicone chips that will get every 10th calculation wrong ..

Appendices

Appendix 1   Advanced Topics – Group Dynamics

A quick look in any Engineering School or Technical Office will tell you that Engineers' inability to interact effectively with non-engineers, and especially with women[117] goes far beyond individual cases and indeed is observed in the majority of engineers. Furthermore, it is an observable, measurable and demonstrably negative phenomenon which adversely impacts not just engineers, but society in general. In short, the world would be a better place to live, for both Engineers and non-Engineers, if Engineers could somehow learn the basic skills required to co-exist with normal humans.

In this context, several philanthropic organisations, supported by generous donations from benefactors and businesses which require more engineers, and occasionally even by government grants, have been investigating the best scientific approach to the problem. This chapter outlines some of the cutting-edge work going on in this fascinating field.

General Observations

It was quickly realised that no amount of training of individual engineers or even groups of engineers could ever provide a satisfactory solution to

---

[117] In line with what we've seen several times previously, women who are also engineers are special cases in relation to this phenomenon too. In what way they are special we cannot specify for legal reasons, but to simplify everyone's life, let's assume that this observation is intended as a compliment. For the rest of this chapter, we therefore let the women engineers glow with pleasure in light of this compliment, and assume that the term "engineer" refers only to male engineers. As stated earlier and often, female engineers will have few difficulties in making the appropriate adjustments to make the analogy work for them in the unlikely event that they should feel any urge to do this.

the problem of engineers' social, and particuarly dating, inadequacies. This is because the core of the problem lies in the fact that engineers do not interact enough with normal people. This problem is both at the heart of their lack of key social skills and an esacerbating factor through which even those few engineers who do have the requisite social skills[118] often do not meet enough potential partners.

It is with this in mind that a significant proportion of the funds invested in improving engineers' social skills has been spent on work in the area of maximizing the extent to which engineers mix with non-engineers.

At the same time, workers are aware of the dangers of letting this situation get out of control. For example, if engineers became aware of the easy, well-paid careers enjoyed by many non-engineers, they might be tempted to switch, resulting in an absence of people who do actual work like produce things, and leading to an eventual economic collapse[119].

Therefore, a parallel project has been going on with the objective of ensuring that, when necessary, it will be possible to safely remove the engineers from among the non-engineers.

In this chapter, we treat first the challenges of generating more intereaction, and then the problem of removal.

In presenting this material, we are very much aware that it is of quite an advanced nature, and potentially beyond even many engineers, with the exception of chemical engineers. Nonetheless, for reasons of completeness, we felt we could not omit it. Readers who find themselves unable to follow this material should not necessarily feel that this reflects poorly on their intellectual capabilities – although, that said, it's probably not something they should speak publicly about either.

Part 1: Promoting Increased Interaction between Engineers and non-Engineers

Before getting into details on the specific challenges and the different requirements of each, let us outline broadly the technical approach to the problem. Chemical engineers have long dealt with the challenge of mixing both compatible and incompatible substances. In the fields of liquid

---

[118] Both of them. [we apologize for this very predictable and cheap attempt at humour – Ed.]

[119] Although this fear has been less emphasised in press coverage than the fear among non-engineers that they may be beset with a plague of engineers of which they would not be able to rid themselves, we feel that, given our target audience, it is best to emphasise the former and downplay the latter.

mixing, these operations are of course easiest where the two liquids are completely mutually soluble, in which case the term "blending" is usually used. Blending creates a mixture that is thermodynamically stable. This can easily be achieved by in-tank agitation, by static mixers in pipelines, or by many other methods, or even by just leaving the two liquids standing around and waiting. The theory is well known and well understood.

However, it's immediately apparent that engineers and non-engineers are non-miscible, with the solubility of engineers among non-engineers being particularly low. For example, even when compressed into a finite volume, such as a staff canteen, one never sees good mixing, but rather clusters of engineers within a continuum of non-engineers. Even if you leave engineers standing around for days, they will show at most minimal mixing with non-engineers.

Indeed, even when some mixing is artificially created, such as by seating engineers and non-engineers at the same tables, a micro-separation quickly occurs as the conversation quickly splits into engineers talking about technical risk analysis and non-engineers talking about Big Brother or Britney Spears. The situation appears dire, and indeed this is the reason why initially so few scientists agreed to work on this project.

Luckily, the problem of mixing immiscible liquids has been studied extensively, and the technology and understanding of the mixing processes involved (typically emulsification[120]) has improved dramatically over the past 20 years or so.

Emulsions are very complex, and even when mixing the same two ingredients, many different final products may be produced depending on how you mix them. However, for simplicity, we will focus on just a few parameters, and clarify the relatively obvious way in which the observations from engineering transform via a process analogous to scale-up into equally valid concepts in the world of dating. We will look at the following key parameters:
- Emulsion creation.
- Emulsion stability
- Emulsifying agents
- Ostwald ripening.

As our readers will be aware, these parameters are very closely interdependent, and these interdependencies too will be seen to be valid in

---

[120] Even the non-technical readers (e.g. Construction Engineers) will be familiar with many emulsions from their daily lives. Mayonnaise is an emulsion of two immiscible liquids – oil and vinegar – and most skin-creams are emulsions of water and non-water-soluble organic compounds.

the world of dating – a concept which raises the interesting possibility of one day running dating experiments in a chemistry lab without needing to go through all that hassle of actually talking to women.

Emulsion creation:
To create an emulsion, you need to supply lots and lots of mixing energy – whether with an industrial scale high-shear mixer or with a whisk, depending on the fluids to be mixed. The reason is that the two phases do not want to mix, and so need to be forced together. The concept is that you can reach a sufficiently small particle size (or droplet size if you prefer) so that the liquids, while still thermodynamically unstable, just can't be bothered separating, because it would take so much trouble to go and look for other droplets. So they hang around long enough for the emulsion to be meta-stable. Frequently an emulsifying agent (a surfactant or hydrotrope) is used to help, making the droplets even less bothered about re-coalescing with their buddies by reducing the (surface) tension between them and the surrounding fluid – and also making the surrounding fluid less dissatisfied with the situation.

Well, I hope that the analogy to mixing women-shy engineers and women is pretty clear in the problem statement. But the challenge is, what is the dating equivalent of a high-shear mixer? How can we create a mixing so intimate that engineers and non-engineers can reach a meta-stable equilibrium?

To mix non-engineers with other non-engineers, where the operation is essentially blending of two compatible groups, low energy applications like discos and bars are sufficient to achieve the desired mixing. But put engineers in a disco, and they'll stand in a corner, too embarrassed to dance or to venture out among people who don't find Laplace Transforms fascinating. Experiments using standard techniques such as discos or bars to mix engineers with non-engineers have proved singularly unsuccessful.[121] At first the failure of these experiments was poorly understood, but Laska, Laska and Laska showed in their classic 2002 paper[122] that these techniques were essentially analogous to in-tank blending with a slow-moving pitch-blade turbine. Furthermore, they showed by numerical simulation that what was needed was a technique which would create singificantly more shear force to break up the groups, as with an SMX[123] static inline mixer or a high-shear (dynamic) mixer.

---

[121] "ChEGS social failuers", UW-Madison Press, 1992.

[122] Laska, J.C, Laska, T.E., Laska, J.D. "Why engineers never pick up cute women in bars – theoretical analysis and practical experiental tests by the author(s)" *AIChEJ* 2002,

[123] Sulzer-Koch static mixer for laminar pipe flows.

Following up on this work, several research projects began. The most promising approach appeared to be the SMX. This works by forcibly dividing a laminar stream of fluid into increasingly narrow strata (see figure), and forcing two or more fluids to come together[124]. Theoretically, an analogous approach to mixing engineers and women, in which the final stratum thickness was roughly equal to the thickness of one engineer (or 1.5 healthy people), would result in effective mixing, where the engineer would be in contact with women roughly in proportion to the relative numbers of engineers and women in the total group. Since frequently engineers will form a minority at social events, this could even result in the engineers being randomly distributed through a large crowd of women, mostly being surrounded by women on all sides.

The authors wanted to test several practical approaches to achieving this, but were unable to find a large group of women willing to participate in the experiment, and so a great opportunity for science was lost.

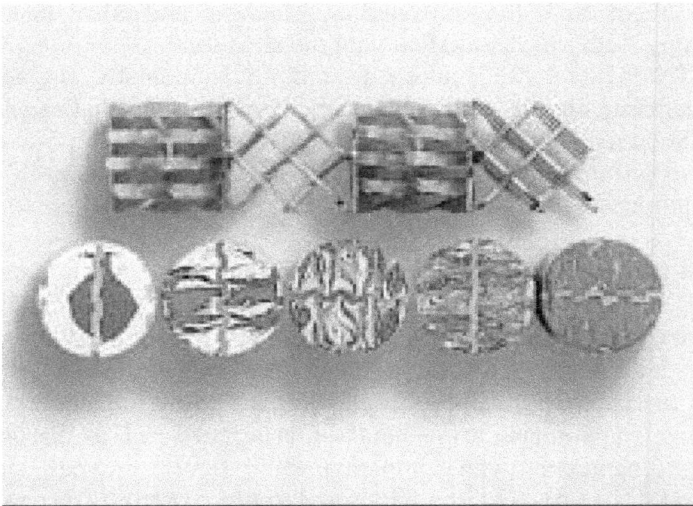

Figure A1.1   How an SMX works. Unmixed white and green fluid flows left to right. The cross-sections show how each stage of the SMX splits the streams into increasingly narrow striations. If you imagine the white to be the engineers standing around the walls, while the green is the non-engineers, and SMX would cause the engineers to be mixed in among the non-engineers, as shown in the diagram. [illustration from Sulzer®].

[124] There was great excitement when this idea was first published until the authors clarified that in this context coming together did not necessarily imply simultaneous orgasm, an admission which killed off the speculation that they were shoo-ins for the Nobel prize.

However, from purely theoretical considerations, several practical approaches can be identified. Any environment with assigned seating, for example a concert or a flight, acts effectively in the manner of a static mixer for a single engineer. There are many events in which the audience is predominantly female, but the engineer must be selective and careful in choosing – for example joining a guided tour of the Impressionist section of the Museum of Modern Art is likely to be more fruitful than attending a Chippendales concert – although any engineer brave enough to try that is encouraged to report his findings to the scientific community.

As we said in the introduction, all this work is ongoing, and as yet few satisfactory mixing techniques have been developed as analogies to high shear mixing (see figure) or even turbulent static mixing. This is unfortunate, in that these techniques tend to be both more effective and more energetic, but application to full-size engineers has proved problematic due to their being significantly larger than the Kolmogoroff scale at which most of the turbulent energy is dissipated. However, there is some wholly unjustified optimism that these difficulties may be tractable, and several unfortunate PhD students have been assigned to spend the next 4 or 5 years basically hoping they get lucky and find a random solution to the problem.[125]

However, being aware that, at least in the laminar case, some simulation is possible, we next turn to the fundamental challenge of emulsion instability:

Emulsion Stability and Emulsifying Agents

For obvious reasons, women don't want to be near engineers if they can help it. And for equally obvious, albeit different reasons, most engineers feel uneasy if they're around women. Therefore, there is a tendency for mixtures of engineers and women to quickly separate into two groups, each feeling mightily relieved that an ordeal has been survived relatively intact.

Technically, this phenomenon is known as emulsion instability, and results from the desire of both the engineers and the women to minimise the intensity of their interactions and return to a more relaxed, lower energy situation. In the field of emulsification, the intensity related to an interaction between two liquids is referred to as the "surface tension" – so that, for example, the surface tension between oil and water is high, and

---

[125] That said, it must be added that they are considerably less to be pitied than some of the Humanities majors who volunteered for the actual testing and "emerged" in the form of suspensions with particle sizes in the range of 1-10 microns – considerably less than the target dimension of just below two meters. With this in mind, we cannot over-emphasise the importance of having any participants in experiments sign full waivers.

this is why they do not mix. Furthermore, even if they are mixed very energetically, they quickly separate into two layers again.

An engineer wishing to mix oil and water in a form that would remain stable would therefore use an emulsifying agent or surfactant. A surfactant is nothing more than a chemical with two halves – one half which likes oil, the other half which likes water. Therefore, when the surfactant is added to the mix, it goes and sits between the water and the oil, with the part that likes the oil (lipophilic) in the oil, and the part that likes the water (hydrophilic) in the water. The result is that suddenly the oil and water are not so unhappy to be beside each other. They will still separate eventually, but this can now take months or years, rather than seconds.

Figure A1.2 A high-shear mixer consists of a stator (on the left) which remains stationary and a rotor (on the right) which rotates at about 10,000 rpm. Initial tests (using Humanities majors) using these devices to mix males and females were successful in the strictly engineering sense of the term, as very intimate mixing was achieved – however, being mixed at a micron-level and emerging as a male/female sausage-consistency fluid was found not to be an acceptable solution for many non-engineers – it was also found that the cost of recruiting volunteers increased significantly after the results of the first trials were published.

So there's clearly hope for the engineer here if an appropriate social emulsifier can be found. The challenge is to find someone or something that is compatible with both engineers and women. And this challenge has proved to be tough.

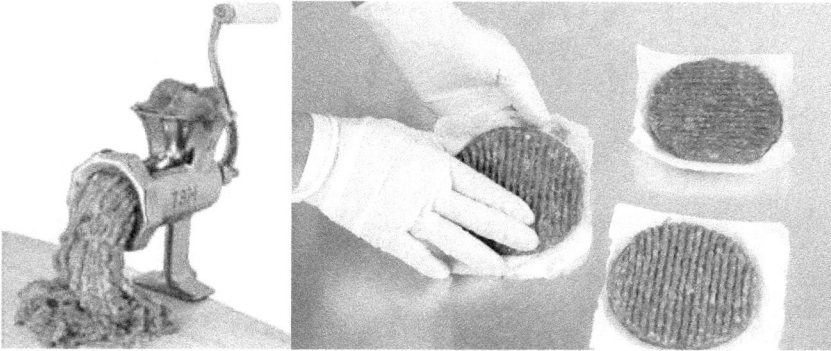

Figure A1.3   Output of homogenisation experiments with male engineers and non-engineering women from studies at the University of Notre Dame (left) and SMU (right). In each case it is seen that an excellent mixing is achieved from a technical point of view, but unfortunately it was impossible to ascertain whether the volunteers themselves were satisfied with the outcome.   When these two studies were presented at the *AIChE* conference in 2002, much was made of the colour difference, and it was at first seen as scientific proof that Catholics and Methodists really are different. In fact, the difference proved to be less religiously interesting – in the Notre Dame study, the engineers had their pocket protectors removed before the homogenisation.   The SMU experiment was finally cancelled after allegations of inappropriate funding surfaced. The photo below shows an item from the SMU campus restaurant taken shortly after the experiment, but for legal reasons we emphasise that we're not making any connection between this hamburger (which sold for $7.99 + tax) and the funding allegations.

Figure A1.4 Hamburger

At first workers used search-engine analysis to identify themes which were frequently searched by both engineers and women. A promising idea, one might surmise. Yet results were disappointing, because it quickly became apparent that even when the item was the same, the concept was so different as to render the interaction meaningless. For example, both women and engineers searched out the term "Ferrari". But there the similarity ended. The women liked the concept of luxury and excitement, and held out some hope of maybe even finding a rich, handsome Ferrari owner who might want to take them on a romantic drive around Toscana. The engineers on the other hand were curious to understand the precise functioning of the engine, the chemical composition of the tyres and the automatic suspension adjustment system. And, worse still, none of the engineers was rich enough to own a Ferrari, so the women were not interested in them.

Similar failures occured with searches for "diamond" (women seemed hardly interested at all in their amazing hardness and cutting ability, but just wanted to wear them!!) and Maria Sharapova (it appears from the typical female queries that she also plays tennis), before this approach was finally given up as unpromising.

The question then arose, could there possibly exist *people* who would be compatible with both women and engineers? It seemed far-fetched, but there was the well known case of women engineers, who were known to be *in*compatible with both groups – therefore, perhaps the matrix-inverse of a woman engineer would be an appropriate emulsifying agent? This field supported at one stage a whole group of post-docs at the University of Maryland, but despite generous incentives, they were unable to find any women engineers willing to be inverted. They did find two volunteers who agreed to be transposed, but this didn't improve their compatibility with either group – as indeed basic theory would have predicted it wouldn't. As a result of the lack of experimental data, the theoretical result remained unproven and of little practical value.

At the University of Auckland, researchers took a different approach. Rather than look for a perfect emulsifying agent from scratch, they reasoned, perhaps it would be better to move one step at a time. They therefore tested various groups along the spectrum between engineers and non-scientific women – for example via a chain of gradually decreasing nerdiness and gradually increasing female-representation.

A typical chain they tested was: engineers, chemists, biologists, psychologists, doctors, economics majors, humanities majors, lingerie models. It was quickly seen that economics majors were of no value[126], and so they were excluded from the study.

Since it was impractical in real terms to imagine a situation where an engineer could be said to be "in contact" with a woman through two or more intermediaries, it was decided that at most one should be used, and so each of the above groups were tested for efficacy, cost-efficiency and odour. It was learned that the chemists were almost as incompatible with women as the engineers – even the women chemists – while psychologists or doctors were already fully incompatible with the engineers. However, with biologists, some hope was seen. The more effective among them were found to be able to sustain a conversation in which there was enough technical content to keep the engineer interested, while at the same time enough human-interest to appeal to the non-technical women. For example, talking about how biochemically engineered pharmaceuticals could help a mommy dog feed her cute little puppies.

However, there was one fatal flaw that killed this idea. While it worked well in laboratory conditions, in real life both engineers and non-engineers agreed that all the biologists they knew personally were morons, and they would not want to be seen in public with them. So this promising work came to an unfortunate, abrubt end.

This is pretty much the current state of knowledge, with no universally accepted solution having been identified and validated. There are a few promising lines of research on-going, but we feel it would be imprudent to publish their preliminary findings at this stage.

---

[126] To avoid any confusion on this point, it should be stressed that there were no qualifiers to this statement, and the conclusion that Economics majors are worthless is generally valid, independently of the context. Once this result was published in the Journal of Economics, it was easy for Engineering researchers to logically prove that, based on this conclusion, Economics Majors would also be worthless in the context of helping engineers interact with women.

Ironically enough, this conclusion has been challenged by a follow-up article in Economics Monthly (which replaced the Journal of Economics after its circulation suddenly and inexplicably declined). In the follow-up article, the authors, Smith and Jackson, claim that the inherent worthlessness of Economics Majors does not necessarily imply that they will be ineffective, only that they will be ineffective in any worthwhile task – and indeed experience confirms their observation that if a task is truly worthless, it is indeed possible that an economist will be relatively good at it.

Therefore, if it can be shown that facilitating interaction between engineers and women is worthless, according to the authors – and many have claimed exactly that – then it is entirely possible that Economics Majors could in fact be helpful in achieving this objective. However, despite this analysis, the decision to remove Economics Majors from the study remained.

Ostwald Ripening

If that conclusion is not depressing enough, it must be remembered that even a solution to that problem would still have to contend with the phenomenon of Ostwald ripening. In a liquid emulsion, this is an additional source of instability resulting from the fact that, on average, more molecules of the dispersed phase will move from small droplets to large droplets than vice versa[127]. The analogy with engineers among women at first appears depressingly obvious, but some researchers actually see hope in this. Let us explain:

Let us consider the case of an emulsion in the early stages of destabilisation, for example what was once 30 engineers randomly dispersed through a group of 150 women has now become three groups of 6 engineers each and four groups of 3 engineers each.[128] Now, Ostwald ripening theory would predict that as time goes one, engineers will gradually move from the groups of three into the groups of six, so that maybe 30 minutes later, there will be three groups of 10 engineers each, at which point their conversation will be entirely engineer-focused and women will be excluded. Even the apparently desirable possibility of being the last engineer in a group and therefore alone surrounded by women doesn't help, as experience shows that that last two engineers will cling onto each other for dear life rather than risk being forced to make small-talk with a group which is totally engineer-less. In practical terms, this means they will move to the larger group together, or else if one leaves, the other will quickly invent an excuse to follow – a phenomenon which I'm sure all our readers have observed.

However, some breakthrough theoretical research at the University of Nevada Las Vegas has brought forward a tantalising idea. If it were possible to somehow destabilise the larger groups, would it it possible to reverse the process, and cause the larger groups to disintegrate rather than coalesce? The process would have to work in such a way that if a group achieved a certain critical mass, it would not grow further and its members would tend to move away from it.

There are two phenomena known which could theoretically work in this way. Where the engineers are students, the effect can be achieved by

---

[127] We could put in the technical explanation for this here and talk about curvature effects in terms of complex tensors or minimisation of the total surface energy of the system, but we know that the only people who'd read it would be those who already understand this and just want the satisfaction of feeling clever – or worse, the satisfaction of contradicting us. Neither of which would serve any valuable purpose in our noble goal of furthering the romantic aspirations of engineers everywhere.

[128] Yes, the total is still thirty, in this analysis we neglect both cannibalisation and murder.

adding one or more Physical Chemistry lecturers to the mix. These sad and lonely men (they're usually men) wander the surface of the globe in search of people who want to listen to their theories about fugacity or when it's appropriate to use the Helmholtz free energy instead of the Gibbs free energy. And even engineers find this extraordinarily dull. The net of these two facts is that, when added to a mix, the lecturers will tend to move towards the largest group of engineers in the room. And while those engineers closest to the lecturer will be forced to stay and listen, those on the outskirts of the group will quickly move away, frequently without even identifying where to go until they've already left the group – so destabilising the large group and creating smaller groups again.

With older engineers who are working in industry, a lecturer does not work so effectively. However, a similar effect can be seen by adding a member of the Quality Assurance program – again this person sincerely wants nothing more than to explain to as many engineers as possible why Quality Assurance is so important and wonderful, and the engineers with whom he or she is talking want nothing more than to violently strangle him or her, or failing that, to kill themselves. But given the social unacceptability of both murder and suicide within the chemical process industry, the effect is usually just that the engineers will move away as quickly as possible from the group – again, counteracting and perhaps even reversing the Ostwald ripening phenomenon.

This approach remains under investigation, but as yet the conclusions presented above are purely theoretical and awaiting experimental validation before further research can be funded.

This survey of the current state of research in mixing engineers and women has necessarily been both brief and depressing. However, despite the many obstacles, there are some pinpoints of light at the end of some very long tunnels, and thus there are many professers happy to have their gradual students waste the best years of their lives studying them.

And with this in mind, there is always the chance that a successful approach will be forthcoming – which renders all the more important, therefore, the second topic in this chapter, namely, how to undo any successful mixing operation before it leads to serious unwanted consequences.

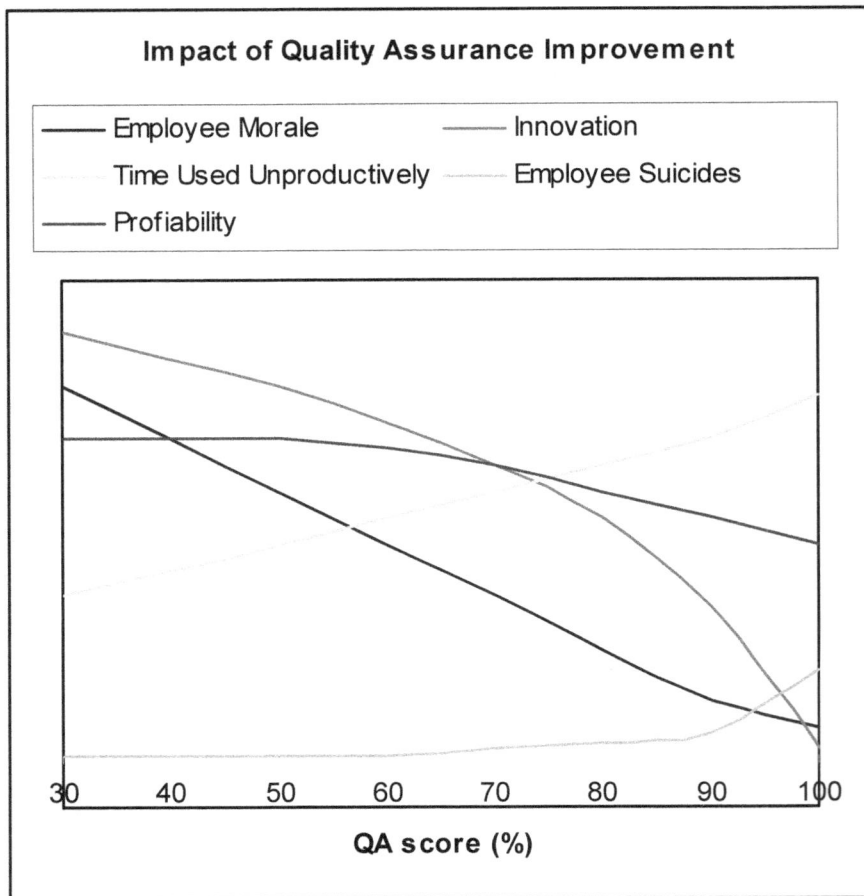

Figure A1.5 While not strictly related to the topic of this book, unless in the sense that suicide and excessive tediousness have been shown to reduce the likelihood of successful interactions with women, it is interesting to note the findings of a recent study carried out by the Gallop organisation which set out to demonstrate the value of Quality Assurance in several large multi-national companies. Innovation is shown to decrease dramatically in highly quality-focused organisations, while suicides and unproductive use of time are seen to rise – resulting in significant profitability loss (to the extent that most PC's are now programmed to refuse to type the word profitability correctly within the context of any QA article in order to limit misinformation of Management by supporters of QA. Unfortunately this doesn't take into account the usual spelling ability of managers). However, these negative outcomes are balanced by the desired impact on employee morale which is shown to drop dramatically as QA compliance increases – a highly successful result for the non-technical functions who see their relative morale compared to those subjected to QA increase dramatically. This effect, which Bunratty calls the "Schadenfreude Phenomenon" is hypothesised to be behind the recent calls by many CEO's for increased QA efficiency in their organisations.

Section 2: Separating Engineers from non-Engineers.

From a technical point of view, this has proved to be a much more tractable problem that the previous one. Admittedly initial researchers made very limited progress due to a flawed assumption: Given that engineers are separate individuals, they chose to look primarily at particulate separation techniques, such as those used in powder separations, and that work yielded few important breakthroughs due to the same technical difficulties which make particle separation such a difficult industrial operation.

However, in a groundbreaking 2001 paper, Dr. Alan Scott of the University College Cork, in Ireland, outlined an approach which would prove much more productive. The technique came from his own specialist discipline of solvent extraction, but resulted not from his laboratory research, but rather from his observations of engineers and non-engineers during college social events.

The basic principle of solvent extraction is that where a component has a significantly higher solubility in one of two immiscible solvents, it is possible to extract that component from the component in which it is less soluble into that in which it is more soluble. The concept is more clearly understood in terms of thermodynamical equations:

Consider a solute, Z, which is initially dissolved in a solvent A. Now consider what happens if another solvent, B, immiscible with A, is added and energetic mixing is applied. If the solute Z is also soluble in B, it will partition between the two phases so that at each interface the chemical potential of Z is equal in the two phases.

$$Z_A \quad \longleftrightarrow \quad Z_B$$

$$\Delta G = \Delta G^0 + RT\, ln(a_Z)_A - RT\, ln(a_Z)_B$$

$$= \Delta G^0 + RT\, [ln(a_Z)_A\, /\, (a_Z)_B]$$

Where G is Gibbs Free Energy and a is activity.

If, for example Z is more soluble in solvent A than in solvent B, this means that its activity coefficient will be higher in the liquid B. Then, if a solution of B containing Z is mixed energetically enough with an equal volume of A, then most of the Z can (eventually) pass from B to A.

The thermodynamics of course gives primarily the equilibrium final concentration only – this will only be achieved if there is sufficient mixing of the two liquids to allow for a large amount of surface area to be created, and if there is sufficient time for diffusion of the Z. Naturally it also depends on the quantities of the two liquids and many other considerations like temperature, pH of the aqueous phase, etc...[129]

The equilibrium concentration of Z can be defined in the form of a partition coefficient. For the sake of this discussion, a simple partition coefficient could be defined as the ratio of concentrations of Z in the two phases at equilibrium:

$$C_{part} = [Z]_A / [Z]_B$$

Using this partition constant, it is easy to calculate the final quantity of Z that will be present in each liquid if the two liquids are first thoroughly mixed and then allowed to separate.

It may not be entirely clear how this situation, however interesting from a purely technical point of view, might be applied to remove engineers from a group of non-engineers. And so, while the theory of solvent extraction had of course been evaluated, it had failed because of the failure of researchers to identify a solvent in which engineers, but not non-engineers, would dissolve. Furthermore, there had been some questions as to whether the need to remove engineers from among non-engineers would ever reach the gravity at which it would be socially and morally acceptable to dissolve them and indeed, much as they might not appreciate engineers as social companions, businessmen were rendered very nervous at the prospect of suddenly having to survive without them, because, as has been mentioned several times in the text, typically, unlike management, they actually do worthwhile work without which production would quickly cease, creating a lack of production which no number of memos or buzzwords could resolve.[130]

Dr. Scott's innovation was the recognition that there existed an organic solvent which could perform the extraction effectively, without the need to

---

[129] In this overview analysis, we will not delve into non-ideal behaviours which can cause these equations to be imprecise. Indeed, given the extent to which the behaviour of engineers in general is non-ideal, this topic alone is currently the subject of several PhD studies. Instead we recognize that the non-ideality will affect the quantitative conclusions in specific cases, but not the qualitative predictions, which remain true.

[130] We apologize for the appalling construction and excessive punctuation in this sentence – it was necessary to render the sentence sufficiently meaningless for it to appear intelligent to business people who might otherwise be offended by it.

dissolve the engineers, and without putting the non-engineers at serious risk. That solvent was ethanol.[131] After running several experiments to estimate the values for the activity coefficients of the engineers among non-engineers and towards the ethanol, (the units of "volume" being per unit non-engineer and per shot of pure ethanol), he found that the technique was potentially very effective. For example, using his data, a random group consisting of 20% engineers by weight would be separated with 70% efficiency[132] in an environment in which a sufficient quantity of ethanol was available. The engineers quickly diffused to the ethanol phase, while then non-engineers mostly did not.

Repeated operation of the separation yielded up to 90% efficiency, but typically no higher, due to some engineers who appeared incompatible with ethanol.[133] However, in most cases this still resulted in the remaining concentration of engineers among the engineers being sufficiently low that most experts considered it safe.

The engineers themselves, whilst freely diffusing towards the ethanol, did not emerge entirely unscathed, and it was found that if the quantity of ethanol available was not controlled, the efficiency of the engineers was greatly reduced for up to 24 hours. However, Dr. Scott was surprised to discover that in spite of these after effects, there were never any problems finding volunteers for his experiments, and the morale of the experimental guinea-pig engineers was exceptionally high. He hypothesised that this was because of the unique situation in which they were able to contribute to the advancement of science not only as theoreticians or experimentalists, but also in the role of participants.

At this time, many workers feel that Dr. Scott's theory has been proven both theoretically and empirically, with strong experimental supporting data. However, Dr. Scott, who frequently participates in his own experiments in order to get a deeper understanding, believes that several hundred more experiments will be necessary to fine-tune the parameters, and he has scheduled experiments on consecutive Friday nights for the

---

[131] How predictable was that?? Unfortunately we're running short on quality original material at this stage …

[132] 70% efficiency in this case means that the concentration of engineers in the non-engineers group could be reduced by 70%, for example from 20% to 6% in this case. The concentration in the primarily engineer group was less concerning, as it has been experimentally shown that removing non-engineers from groups of engineers is a trivial operation which usually occurs spontaneously – when it does not, it can easily be initiated by starting a conversation on the subject of the merits and demerits of different computational risk-analysis algorithms in the design of electricity generation plants.

[133] He observed two types of incompatibility. The first type was permanent incompatibility, which was quite rare among engineers. The second type was temporary, and appeard especially important if a similar extraction had been performed within the previous 24 hour period.

next 9 years. This work is all being generously supported by a grant from the Arthur Guinness foundation.

Conclusion

At this point, the work on mixing engineers with non-engineers is still not at a point where we can truly predict when a workable solution will be found – however, it does appear likely that at least the related problem of how to achieve separation if and when desired, is more tractable.

We hope to give a more encouraging discussion of this work in our next edition.

Appendix 2: Introduction to Statistics and the Null Hypothesis

---

This article is the point at which most non-engineers got irrevocably confused with statistics and decided to place their trust in mysticism and faith-healers instead. Since this idea recurs frequently in this book, we will explain it here in language that even a lawyer could understand:

Let's say you want to prove that people whose name is Brian are on average taller than furry green martians, by measuring a sample of furry green martians and Brian's (but not all of them!!), and comparing their heights. The following considerations arise:

1. You cannot prove this with statistics. You can never prove anything with statistics unless you measure 100% of the sample, in which case it's sort of pointless to use statistical inference. This is perfectly in line with reality, since no matter how many you measure, you don't know for sure that there aren't any furry green martians who are 8' tall hidden under the surface laughing their asses off while silly space-ships try to detect life in the form of dead microbes.

2. The best you can ever do is demonstrate, with stated assumptions and probability theory, that it's incredibly likely that this is the case.

3. The way that you demonstrate this (or anything) with statistics is to state the *opposite* conclusion as a hypothesis (the "null hypothesis"), and demonstrate that your data (in this case height measurements) are incredibly unlikely to occur if your null hypothesis is true. In other words, *the null hypothesis is the opposite of what you want to prove*. However, even the "opposite" here can confuse people. If you want to claim that Brian's are taller than furry green martians, statistically this is saying two things:

- There is a difference in average height between Brian's and furry green martians
- The difference is that Brian's are typically taller. The other possibility (for the philosophy students reading this) is that they might be shorter.

However, the key point is, your null hypothesis is the opposite of the first statement – namely it says that there is no difference in average height between Brian's and furry green martians.

So, to prove that Brian's are taller than furry green martians, you proceed as follows:

1. state your null hypothesis "Brian's are on average the same height as furry green martians".
2. collect lots of data, let's say the heights of 200 Brian's and 200 furry green martians. (At this point, we could get even more dull by discussing the importance of quality experimental design and making sure that your furry green martians would not only exist, but also be available for measurement in your laboratory and be representative of the population of furry green martians. But we won't.)
3. run a statistical test to measure the likelihood that the two data sets are random choices from the same population. What does that mean? To simplify, let's look at a group of 5 furry green martians and 5 Brian's.

Brians	furry Green martians
5'11	5'0
6'2	5'1
5'5	5'4
5'9	5'6
6'0	5'3

Now, plot these on a line:

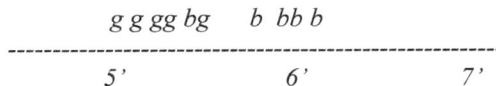

```
       g g gg bg   b bb b
     ------------------------------------------------
        5'              6'              7'
```

Even if you had no idea what these numbers meant, if I told you that these were ten randomly chosen numbers from a "population" which averaged about 5'6, you would not believe me. It would seem to you that there were two different populations – the b's which might be random choices from a population averaging about 5'10 and the g's which might be random choices from a population averaging about 5'3. It's obvious that the b's and the g's don't come from the same random population, you'd say. In fact, statistics will not tell you it's obvious, they will just tell you that it's incredibly unlikely. And they will tell you exactly how unlikely it is. They will tell you something like "It is 99% certain that the b's and the g's come from different populations". At some stage in the future between when I'm writing this and when you're reading it, we'll probably put in an appendix to explain all this with mathematical precision – but if you grasp the concept and are willing to trust us to do the math, you'll be able to understand most of the probability derivations in this book.

This example is extremely trivial, but there may be some chemists reading this book (the more literate chemists obviously), so we'll do an even simpler example, stolen from Tom Stoppard. In the play "Rosencranz and Guildenstern are Dead", one of the two flips a coin 160 or so times, and it comes up tails every time. How would we use this data to prove that the coin is biased?

If you've understood the above example, you'll know that you can't prove it. All you can say is "if the coin is not biased, or two-tailed, then it's incredibly unlikely that someone would flip it and get tails 160 times in a row – incredibly unlikely, but not impossible."

And when you apply this logic to your own life, you will reach two simple conclusions:

1. It's very likely that there is a bias in my life which is preventing me from getting laid as often as I would like.

2. As soon as I remove this, or better yet, reverse it, it's likely I will get laid a lot more often.

Of course the flipside if this is that if you didn't understand the above example, you're likely already benefitting from the incredibly strong correlation between lack of statistical understanding and frequent sex.

Appendix 3   Note from Greta and Gertrude

Gentle Reader,

We discovered too late that our photo was being used, without our permission, in this book (see page 32 – Ed). A quick analysis of the authors' bank accounts revealed that suing them was unlikely to yield the type of income that would make it worthwhile following up, and a quick look at the book confirmed that there was no likelihood that they were going sell enough copies to make a share of the royalties interesting either.

So instead, we negotiated to write a preface[134] which would clearly outline our moral repulsion at the content of this book, our unmitigated cynicism as to the practical benefits the authors claim the text offers, and our general personal disapprobation of the authors per se (even though we only know one of them).

While we can't say we ever found the authors' romantic disappointments particularly surprising, reading this book, or at least reading as much as we could before getting bored, which wasn't much, has given us a deeper understanding than before of why it is that one of them is still single, while the other has had to marry a German.

---

[134] While respecting the wishes of all parties, including the writers of the appendix, it was deemed that putting this at the front of the book would possibly have a negative impact on sales. We, the publishers, found Pope Innocent's preface to be significantly more helpful in this context – although it must be admitted that this appendix is somewhat more precise in its evaluation of the book and its usefulness to society in general.

Indeed, if they have been using these techniques, it amazes us that either of them has ever had a date in his entire life. And while some of the sexual techniques suggested might be interesting, the authors might like to consider applying these in combination with more traditional techiques like flowers, chocolates and dinners in nice restaurants with white tablecloths.

There is much more we could write, about wit and charm and opening doors and dressing well, but we fear that adding any useful content might only increase sales of the book, with the result that our association, albeit totally undesired and almost certainly illegal, would be seen by even more people.

Therefore, we strongly encourage you and plead with you not to buy this book. And if you have bought it, we suggest that you burn it immediately, lest its very presence on your shelves, or indeed, even in the darkest recessess of your attic, create an image which surely you would not want people to take away, and which might significantly reduce the value of your home should you ever choose to sell it.

Thank You

Gertrude and Greta[135]

---

[135] Not our real names, for obvious reasons.

Appendix 4:   Understanding Engineers for non-Engineers[136]

Engineers tend to have a very practical, but frequently misguided view of the world. The following tales might help clarify how the engineering mind works. The stereotypical engineer is assumed to be male ..

Two engineering students were biking across a university campus when one said, "Where did you get such a great bike?"
The second engineer replied, "Well, I was walking along yesterday, minding my own business, when a beautiful woman rode up on this bike, threw it on the ground, took off her clothes and said, "Take what you want."
The second engineer nodded approvingly and said, "Good choice; the clothes probably wouldn't have fit you anyway."

To the optimist, the glass is half full.
To the pessimist, the glass is half empty.
To the engineer, the glass is twice as big as it needs to be.

A priest, a doctor and an engineer were waiting behind a particularly slow group of golfers.
The engineer fumed, "What's with those guys? We've been waiting 15 minutes!"
The doctor chimed in, "I don't know, but I've never seen such inept golfers!"
The priest said, "Here comes the greenkeeper, let's ask him."

---

[136] We apologize that we were not able to find the original sources of any of these, which are mostly vague recollections of jokes or ideas we thought were funny when we were in college, even though nobody else laughed when we told them ..

He said, "Hello, Mike! What's up with the group ahead of us? They're very slow, aren't they?"

The greenkeeper replied, "Oh, yes. That's a group of blind firefighters. They lost their sight saving our clubhouse from a fire last year, so we always let them play for free anytime."

The group fell silent for a moment.

The priest said, 'That's so sad. I think I will say a special prayer for them tonight."

The doctor said, "Good idea. I'm going to contact my ophthalmologist colleague and see if there's anything he can do for them."

The engineer said, "Why can't they play at night?"

Four graduates were in a restaurant talking about the latest electronic gadget that was taking the country by storm. The Science graduate said, "I wonder why it works". The Engineer said, "I wonder how it works." The Accountant wondered "How do the make a profit on it?" The Marketing graduate asked "And do you want fries with your order?"

Normal people believe that if it ain't broke, don't fix it. Engineers believe that if it ain't broke, it doesn't have enough features yet.

An engineer was crossing a road one day, when a frog called out to him and said, "If you kiss me, I'll turn into a beautiful princess."

He bent over, picked up the frog and put it in his pocket.

The frog spoke up again and said, "If you kiss me and turn me back into a beautiful princess, I will stay with you for one week."

The engineer took the frog out of his pocket, smiled at it and returned it to his pocket.

The frog then cried out, "If you kiss me and turn me back into a princess, I'll stay with you for one week and do ANYTHING you want."

Again the engineer took the frog out, smiled at it and put it back into his pocket.

Finally, exasperated the frog asked, "What is the matter with you? I've told you that I'm a beautiful princess and I'll stay with you for one week and do anything you want. Why won't you kiss me?"

The engineer said, "Look, I'm an engineer. I wouldn't know what to do with a girlfriend, but a talking frog, now *that's* cool."

www.ingramcontent.com/pod-product-compliance
Lightning Source LLC
Chambersburg PA
CBHW030929090426
42737CB00007B/370